Apple of My I
The Four Practices of Self-Love

Tools for authentic living in a chaotic world

Yudit Maros

Learn to love yourself for a happy, joyful and sober life!

BALBOA
PRESS

A DIVISION OF HAY HOUSE

Balboa Press books may be ordered through booksellers or by contacting:

Balboa Press
A Division of Hay House
1663 Liberty Drive
Bloomington, IN 47403
www.balboapress.com
1 (877) 407-4847

Printed in the United States of America.

ISBN: 978-1-4525-9795-9 (sc)
ISBN: 978-1-4525-9794-2 (e)

Balboa Press rev. date: 11/24/2014

This book will affect the lives of millions in a profound, private and lasting way. Yudit Maros shares a great gift: a life changer upon first read, her book becomes a daily guide with repeated openings of its pages. These steps toward wholeness are helpful for yogis to bring their practice off the mat, voyagers and the laypeople alike. Apple of My I will help you to find your way back to yourself, guaranteed!

Tiffany Chion, Owner, Yoga Universe

Yudit Maros has created an amazing healing resource. This book is FANTASTIC! I am getting a copy for everyone I love.

Beverly Stantial, Life Coach

After reading this book, for the first time in my life I can be sad and not feel like I am suffering. That's a distinction I never understood before. Everything isn't perfect, but with the help of this method I feel more and more grounded every day. I'm making very different choices than I have in the past, choices that reflect better self-respect and self-care. I feel more in control and am confident that I have a happy future ahead.

Julie Revaz, LCSW

Yudit Maros has written a personal, heartfelt and reader-friendly guide to healing. She guides us gently along a path she has walked herself and now invites us to join her in our search for ourselves.

Gabor Maté M.D.

Author of When The Body Says No: Exploring The Stress-Disease Connection

To my parents Verus and Gyuri, who loved me well.

Contents

Acknowledgements

It took the vision, wisdom and skill of a lot of people in two different countries for this book to come to fruition. Here, I want to thank them all for their contribution and good will, hoping to include everyone.

Christine (Farber), you gave me the initial validation and encouragement when you took an interest in this work in its germinal stages: you were instrumental in opening the door to the wider professional audiences. Thank you Cathy (DePorte) for your friendship and consistent faith in me and my inquiries. Where would I be without you and your inspiration? Roxy (Furman), your linguistic skills saved the day when I tried to tackle this complex material in my fourth language.

Your undying generosity of spirit, Nancy (Gordon-Green), helped me through many a hurdle in the decade it took to accomplish this work. Many thanks to you, Tom (Levine) for your insights about how to frame my ideas, and to you, Ilona (Sakalauskas) for suggesting helpful ways to bring the message home.

Aniko (Kocsis), my friend and translator, I so appreciate your experience infused with open heartedness; and I thank you, Feri (Vicsek) for your expert advice along the way. Warren (Grossman), your seemingly stern initial feedback opened my eyes to the virtues of simple delivery – thank you!

My gratitude goes out to all my clinician friends who took my workshops and game me invaluable feedback as well as validation. You were – and are – the mirror and the open forum where this new approach has been allowed to flourish and spread. A heartfelt thanks also to the Hungarian clinicians who created the Association for Authenticity Therapy, and who are at the forefront of this new psychology.

I am eternally grateful to my clients over the decades; none of this work would have been possible without the gift of their on-going trust and candidness.

I do not know where I would be without my family: Peter, my husband, and Julia, Peter, and Beanie. You refill my love-tank each day for the energy I need to work, and to be joyful.

Introduction

If I am not for myself, who will be for me?

And if I am only for myself, what am I?

If not now, when?

Hillel

"Be true to yourself" – too bad the old adage does not come with a user's manual. Yet, modern psychology corroborates the truth of popular wisdom: we are happiest and healthiest when we follow our inner guidance. It is not easy however to do something when you don't know *how*. I wrote this book to offer up just that: a user-friendly manual to living an authentic life, one true to who you really are. Experience shows that when you live this way inner peace and happy relationships follow closely.

Authenticity has a prerequisite, however: accepting and loving one's Self. Indeed, why would you follow your inner guidance if it came from someone you don't trust, or care about?

If there is one thing I learned in over two decades of practicing psychotherapy it is this: the way we feel about and treat ourselves is the blueprint beneath all of what we experience – and create – in our lives. While assisting people go from pain to well-being, from suffering to peace, I came to realize that nothing impacts our lives more than the level to which we accept and love our own Selves. Every segment, every layer of our existence is a direct extension of that underlying relationship, a mirror image of it. I now firmly believe that *the only way to be well and good to others is to love one's Self.*

What is love? Common perception would equate it with kindness, compassion and care. Love is most promptly observable in the way parents relate to their children in a healthy family. What we see is a rich complexity of stances, actions and behaviors that run the gamut from positive attention, acceptance, compassion, soothing, to listening, expressing affection, setting limits, being available to help, guidance, advocacy, and in general doing what it takes for the child to be well. Clearly, love is *a lot* more than a good, warm feeling.

I see my job as a therapist as helping my clients to learn to love and help themselves, and to give themselves all that a good parent would offer. I do this by guiding them back to their own selves, to their inner guidance: the body's wisdom. Here, on these pages I will show you how you too can learn to make peace within, between what you think, and how you feel. As you learn to synchronize your mind with your body you will be ready to commit to parent yourself with love and acceptance, which truly is the ultimate goal of a life well lived.

A life built on inner guidance, i.e. an authentic life requires self-love. Consider for a moment how you would treat someone you truly love: that is the way you must learn to treat yourself in words, actions and attitudes. When you look at it this way, you can see that self-love has nothing to do with narcissism, grandiosity, or selfishness, just like you would not judge a child for needing love. As a mature and healthy person you must be both the giver and the receiver of such love, from you to you.

This inner connection is what enables us to be happy and healthy. We could not recognize love, acceptance, and care from others, even if it was staring us in the face, if we did not first create this within. Every aspect of our lives – relationships, work, and circumstances - is an extension of how we relate to our Selves, a mirror image of the way we treat ourselves.

I will introduce you to the Authenticity Process: a guide to create or deepen a positive, loving connection with your inner Self, so that you may manifest and generate health and wellbeing for you *and* for others. This is the practice of self-love. As we shall see, it is steeped in an understanding that the body speaks the truth, and nothing but the truth. The process consists of four steps that enable us to listen to the body and translate its messages without any alterations.

Focusing primarily on your body means calling on the carrier of the only person you can truly know and help: You. During this process you may get a lot of insight as to the how's and why's of what you see manifesting in your life. Chances are, old patterns will become clear, and connected with what is happening to you today.

Is this book for you? I believe it is for *everyone*. Who could not use more self-love, more harmony within? Still, you will especially benefit from reading and using the four-step Authenticity Process if you often feel frustrated, tired, powerless, sad, lonely, empty or anxious, perhaps because of repeating old, destructive patterns in your life. It will also help if you suffer from low self-esteem, low self-confidence, lack of joy or energy, emotional numbness, or if you are often critical or judgmental of yourself. This approach will also be helpful if you have a tendency to doubt your feelings or struggle to make decisions. Feeling stressed, overwhelmed, angry, desperate, or burned out? Suffering from physical aches and pains? In short, if you feel at odds or out-of-synch with yourself in *any way* read on!

Another way to see how well this book is suited for you is determining the degree to which you generally experience inner peace and happiness: if it is, say, a 6 or less on a scale from 0 (none) to 10 (all), read on. Chance are, here you will find ways to tweak it up to 8 or more. The point is: always reach for better! Even if you would never go to a doctor or a psychotherapist, you do not have to lead a lackluster existence.

There is help!

Life can be a lot better, as long as you know what you can do to help yourself.

In the first half of this book you will find the answers to why you should love and accept yourself, and we shall debunk some sturdy, old myths and beliefs that may stand in the way of your self-care.

Part One is an introduction to the basic elements of an authentic, i.e. healthy life.

Part Two will address and clarify any misconceptions, correct any beliefs that might be in your way – and hopefully, talk you out of them! As a result, you will be ready to fully commit to accepting your own feelings as your best guidance, your "true north", and thus, to make the four steps a way of life.

In Part Three, we will explore the main principles of positive self-parenting and you will be able to identify your current self-parenting style.

Finally, in Part Four, you will find a detailed explanation of the four fundamental practices of self-love, along with the skills necessary to perform them. These four practices are the ABCD's of health: Attention, Breath, Communication, and Delivery, which, performed consistently constitute what is both necessary and sufficient to live in alignment with one's inner truths. As these practices become your automatic pilot you will be parenting yourself with love, a prerequisite for mental and physical health that leads to safe and close relationships.

Toward the end of the book, you will meet "Shrinkster", a quick technique that can serve as your personal emotional health assistant. Like a "shrink in your pocket" Shrinkster is a shortened version of the four practices that will always be there to help you feel better in a pinch. But please, do not jump to Shrinkster hoping to find a "quick fix". It is a distilled version of a complex self-parenting method, and you must give yourself time to hone the skills involved in it. In order to ensure that this quick version of self-help will truly deliver, it must be built on a good month's period of daily practice of the exercises involved in the full four-step process.

I welcome you on this journey. This may be your most amazing ride; it carries the potential to transform your life, bringing you joy and peace. With the help of these practices you will feel better and better – as you can see, I am giving it to you in writing. Your chalice will be filled up, day in and day out with positive energy, and radiance. Then, you will be able to pour it onto the people in your life in a way that is sustainable. In truth, we can only transcend what we have inhabited once, and thus, *the road to selflessness leads through embracing the Self.*

My Story

Love yourself? Trust your body? Deplorably, and despite my profession, this was outside of even my peripheral vision. Always busy and distracted, I, like many others, had been living in a profound disconnect from, and mistrust of myself, my own feelings – and did not even know it! There was always so much to do: I was immersed in creating a new life in a new country, while also raising a family. This must have gone on for about a decade – and then, while on vacation in Maine, when the freight train of my life came to a temporary halt - my heart literally began to shoot pain signals, and in a frighteningly quick succession. Needless to say, that got my attention! My mother died of a heart attack at 62, and I was *not* going to go down that path. That is when I started to listen to my body.

I knew this was big. I asked my husband to leave me there, on the seashore; I felt an irresistible urge to be alone and tune inwards. As I paid attention to the pain, I was flooded with reprimands from my inner self: "You never listen to me! I am tired! I feel lonely! I need more friends! I need to have more fun! Get me a hobby! Where is my community?" It was shocking, and humbling how my body knew, while *I did not have a clue* about the many ways I had been deprived. This experience set the stage for some well overdue changes.

Being yelled at by myself happened on the tail end of a long, painful burnout, where I felt exhausted and despondent most of the time. I had a thriving private practice, and the word on the street was that I was successful at helping my clients. I was oblivious to the sad fact that by then for a while work was all I could muster energy for. I got used to living like an empty satchel, a giver who never received. This run-in with myself in Maine was what brought it all home to me. It taught me the long-overdue lesson that I must begin to pay attention to my body and give myself what I need. I had to start loving myself better (and I thought I did!). When my heart was shooting pain signals, exasperating as it felt I came to realize that it actually saved my life. How? By getting my attention.

I have to add that sometime before this, another thing hit me over the head. One day, over lunch, a colleague asked me about my "angle" in therapy - and I was dumbfounded. For the life of me, I could not articulate it! "I don't know... but it works!" – I stuttered. Later that day I began to feel a slow simmer of shame: how come I didn't know *exactly* what happened in my therapy sessions that was helpful? That did not sit right with me; I am not an amateur, this is inadmissible! Two titans of emotions clashed in me: the pride I took in being a good therapist, and the shame of not knowing how I did it. I *had to* get to the bottom of this!

I guess this was my time to get to the bottom of what healing is all about in general – whether for myself, or for others.

From that day forward, with an open mind and heart, I made it my calling to find out just that. I had a burning desire to know what the underlying reasons are for unhappiness, or, conversely, what makes for a happy life. Is there a system, an order behind the chaos of the stories and the myriad variations of human experience I was witnessing, and behind the just as many stories of healing? There *had to be* some organizing factor, a common pattern invisibly operating in the background, I was convinced of it! Like a maniac, I took notes of anything that people found helpful in our work together, and once in a while (when the piles of scrap paper were threatening to collapse) funneled all the information into its common denominators.

Determined not to interfere with anything that emerged, I snuffed all preconceptions, all expectations, other than some type of a coherent order. As I was patiently chiseling information down to its simplest elements what slo-o-o-owly emerged (in the span of three-four years) was that the one place where our truths – and healing - reside is *the body*. This caught me by surprise; I never expected to go that "deep", that far away from my familiar grounds of left-brain knowledge about the psyche, that our brains control our lives, and that the mind is where it all is at. I remember instances where I got glimpses of this truth-in-body notion: one time I said to a woman to just tell her husband how she felt. She looked at me, startled, and told me she does not know how she feels, and would I please tell her how she could find that out? All the invisible arrows around us were pointing to her body, even then. The moment she focused on her body the feeling words just flew off her lips, for the first time for him – or even her! - to hear.

Over time, four common denominators emerged, four factors that determine the degree of a person's health. My decade of experience probing this method shows that together they are both necessary and sufficient to achieve and maintain health: attention to the body's sensations, soothing oneself with them, so we may be informed by those sensations about our feelings and needs, and use their guidance to take action to help ourselves. At the foundation of this whole process is the body with its instantaneous signals of discomfort to alert us when help is needed.

These four factors looked vaguely familiar: isn't this what they call love? Hmm... could this be how love heals? It gradually dawned on me that our health depends on the degree to which one receives these salves. From where? It does not matter. Anywhere - but first and foremost, from one's Self.

The Authenticity Method

In this book you will find the distilled essence of my clinical and personal experience. In the past decade or so, since I have been using this method my work's effectiveness has multiplied. I believe this is so because the Authenticity Method zeroes in on the core issue in emotional – as well as general - health: *how you relate to your feelings.*

I wrote this for the people on the streets who often struggle with family issues, job problems, as well as their own Selves, their feelings. I wanted it to be easily accessible for everyone, without the added – or rather underlying – layer of the different psychological theories and practices that informed this work, so that this tool may reach the masses of people who need it the most. I have also been offering trainings to psychotherapists (both in Europe and in the US) in an effort to disseminate Authenticity Therapy for the effective and powerful tool it is in helping people heal.

It might help here to give you an overview of the way things stand today in the field of mental health care in the United States. We have at least seven different professions practicing psychotherapy, from dozens of different angles. LPC's, LMFT's, LCSW's, Ph.D.'s, Psy. D.'s, M.D.'s M.Div.'s, APRN's utilize multiple perspectives and schools of thought that are all legitimate and helpful in their own way: Systemic, Psychodynamic, Experiential, Gestalt, Narrative, Somatic, Transactional, Cognitive-Behavioral, Dialectical Behavioral, and Emotionally Focused are but a few of the angles used in helping people with emotional and relational issues.

Authenticity Therapy is an umbrella framework, a synthesis that organizes and streamlines the best practices and traditions of psychological thinking from a new angle. It is based on the observations that the body carries all the information necessary for meeting our needs, and it communicates through sensation. The Authenticity Method is a four step protocol by which one can tap into that information, and then translate the signals of sensation into healthy action.

When it comes to building and maintaining emotional health – or happiness – there is a clear sequence of events:

1. you can only be well to the degree to which you get what you need;
2. you can only get what you need if you reach for it;
3. you can only reach for what you need if you know what it is;
4. you can only realize what it is, if you pay attention to your body;
5. you can only pay attention to your body if you are able to focus on it;
6. you can only focus on your body if you feel safe doing so;
    (You can only feel safe focusing on your body if you don't carry body memory of trauma; If you carry body memory of trauma, like being a victim of abuse or neglect - you can tell by repeating destructive patterns of thinking and behavior and choices, despite of you knowing better - you must get help to extinguish it from your body's programming with a body-centered therapy. EMDR (Eye Movement Desensitization and Reprocessing), or BSTOR (Brief, Solution Oriented Trauma Resolution) can be helpful.)
7. When you focus inward you can learn new ways of coping with stress – both in thought and actions - with the help of AT (Authenticity Therapy), or CBT (Cognitive Behavioral Therapy), or DBT (Dialectical Behavior Therapy), or any other modality that emphasizes skill-building.

Your New, or rather your True Self will emerge as this work goes on, along with a renewed sense of joy and happiness.

The Authenticity Method offers the tasks (e.g. loving, accepting, soothing and helping yourself), and the most essential tools (e.g. focusing, relaxing, assertiveness) for re-building one' life after traumas have been resolved. It is like psychoanalysis on steroids, or a sort of turbo-Freudism for self-help: you get the tools to drill to the core of what ails you, but in a matter of minutes, not years. This is because you ask directly the one and only authority on what is true for you: your body. Once you know the truth of how you feel and what you need to feel better, you will be poised to reach for just that. There is no fat to be trimmed here, it is as straightforward and simple as that. I will show you how, right here, on these pages.

PART ONE

What is Self-Love?

If you would love yourself
You would never harm another.
Buddha

Love is Spelled A-B-C-D

Slowly it became evident that we all do better or worse depending on how well we pay attention to our needs, and get them met. Just like any living organism we are well to the degree to which our needs are fulfilled.

But don't go searching for what you need in your mind: needs are not what you *think*: they live in your body. Reach for them, and ask for what you cannot reach or walk to. When, and how, you might ask? The moment your body informs you *through sensation*. It does so each moment, pointing us to what is good and healthy, to what will make us happy now, as well as in the long run. The body is our best friend: it never lies, and it will *always* guide us into the next healthy action. If and when we listen to it, that is.

Here is a quick rundown of the ABCD's of how to listen to you internal guidance system, and thus re-establish, and maintain health:

A is for Attention to your body's signals, and Acceptance of them;

B stands for Breath and self-soothing with the discomfort of those signals;

C means Communication with those signals, and then, with others about how you feel and what you need to feel better, and

D is for - you guessed it - Doing (or Delivering) what you found out, what it takes to feel better.

As I mentioned, in the second half of this book I will offer you a deeper understanding of these steps, and introduce you to the practices involved in their performance. For now, massage yourself into trusting your body's sensations as the conveyors of the highest truth there is: your own. The body is chuck full of vital information: all you need to do is read it and follow its guidance.

The four steps are easy to remember, simple to perform, and you will learn all the skills involved in being able to perform them. Together, they form the most powerful self-help tool imaginable, a veritable upward cycle of ever-improving health. This is because only *you* have access to Nature's information about what you need to be well. Therefore, only *you* can take care of yourself. When you take primary responsibility for your own health and balance, and you know what to do, you cannot help but help yourself, and thus be well.

You can use this method in any situation; it will ensure that your actions are based on your inner truths. What better way to be in this world than to be true to yourself, to be authentic? How about doing this all day long – not instead, but *while* you are engaged in any activity or conversation, in real time? It is like having ongoing, free access to the wisest guru there is! And for free! As you make these skills your own, and practice each day, they will come to you automatically, becoming your second nature. You will then experience the above mentioned upward spiral of health and well-being in your life.

I owe it to the four practices described in this book that I gradually became the "apple of my eye", and regained my health and energy. Since I was pretty far gone, it took me a few years to come back from the burnout. In turn, I owe it to you to share what I know to be true.

I think of this book as a bouquet of four beautiful flowers for you. Each of them carries tremendous healing power, and together they will transform your life, like they have already transformed the lives of thousands of people who use them.

What's In Your Head?

There are a few pretty common myths and misconceptions that get in the way of delivering the seemingly simple task of loving one's Self. Here is a compilation of some of the most common thoughts and persuasions that may do more harm than good when it comes to self-acceptance and self-love. Check the box next to the statement that applies to you:

- I cannot love or care for myself if no one else does
- I don't know how to love myself – I never did
- Feelings don't matter
- Feeling bad is selfish (or lazy, self-indulgent, negative)
- Feelings are unimportant: what matters is what you think/do
- I don't want to feel sorry for myself
- I don't know how I feel
- I don't want to feel and then hurt even more!
- I don't know what I need
- I don't know how to give myself what I need
- It's selfish to reach for what I need
- I have difficulty asking for what I need
- People don't listen to what I need
- I don't believe I can get what I need in life
- I don't want to whine or be negative– I have it good!
- I don't like/trust my body or myself
- I had a terrible childhood, I am done for
- When I trust my body it tells me to drink/do drugs/avoid situations
- My mind won't shut off
- My mind is negative, and won't let me reach for what I need
- What if my family/friends/neighbors/colleagues will not like me if I put myself first?
- I don't have time/energy/will to put myself first
- I have no control over my life

- □ I am afraid to look inside of me: what if I don't like what I see?
- □ Being authentic is a luxury I don't have
- □ Am I worth all this?
- □ _____(Fill in the blank)

Let us now, together, peel back the layers that cover up your self-loving core. I understand that you believe the things you checked off (if you did not put a check next to anything, good for you!) But please know that just because we believe something that does not make it true. We believe it, because we have been told, and shown something repeatedly over time. We are learning machines, and with insistent repetition we get it – and then, continue to repeat (through words and actions) the same messages to ourselves, thus effectively perpetuating that belief. This, even long after the situation that created the belief is gone! We forge beliefs because we learn from repetition, but also to cope with situations. Once those situations or conditions are gone the beliefs remain, outdated, obsolete, a wrench in the forward moving evolution of your spirit. As such, they must be removed so that you may grow and heal.

My Dear Reader, the exercises in this book are good quality "mental flosses". Use them daily, to get rid of the "plaque" blocking you from clarity, health and balance.

Am I Worth It?

I believe our overarching common experience as humans is this:

Sooner, or later,
> *one way or another,*
>> *through love or through pain*
>>> *we are all taught that we matter.*

Be a good student, and you will hurt less.

Many people grow up feeling less than loved, which leaves one feeling unworthy of love. You must remember that whatever others give you (at any age), whatever they do or say, is about *them* and not about *you*. If your parents and your family fell short in making you feel good about yourself, that does not mean *you* do not deserve it; it only means that *they* could not. In fact, they did not give it to themselves either, meaning they did not have it to give in the first place.

Anything that tells you that you are not worthy of love is by definition a fallacy. Anyone who tells you that you are less than is by definition wrong. You were born because you are worthy to live. Nature does not waste any energy – and look at how long of a gestation, how much preparation goes into a baby being born! You are born to bring your unique energy into this world, the one only you can contribute. The only way you can realize this mandate is if you are well – which, again, is only possible if you get what you need.

You see, every baby is born with no qualms about whether or not he should be getting what he needs – that is a given. Any belief in your way of asking for what you need, that is lovingly taking care of yourself is born out of certain circumstances and life experiences, more specifically abuse, neglect, or trauma. By now, however, all that is probably gone, and along with them the tools you used to survive and cope must go as well: your negative beliefs about your worth. You now have the choice to stop letting them rule your life. Abuse, neglect and trauma are "outlier" experiences, not what we consider healthy or normal (even if they are the norm in your surroundings). The conclusions you might have drawn from them must be re-formulated in order for you to be able to effectively commit yourself to living and cultivating self-love that is unquestionable and sustainable.

Did your experiences as a young person give you doubts about your right to be alive and well, or about who is in charge of your life? If so, the following chapters will help you to reconsider, and help you settle the issue once and for all:

1. *You have the right to be well;*
2. *You are the boss of your life.*

As you become more and more persuaded of this, you will have no difficulty paying attention to and helping yourself. *Awareness of how you feel as you go through the day is the very cornerstone of health.* The way you treat yourself defines how you relate to others as well, how much attention, kindness, and presence you are able to offer up in the world. Being compassionate with yourself is truly the greatest gift you can give to others.

YOU: Your Greatest Ally

In dwelling, live close to the ground.
In thinking, keep to the simple.
In conflict, be fair and generous.
In governing, don't try to control.
In work, do what you enjoy.
I family life, be completely present.

When you are content to be simply yourself
And don't compare or compete,
Everybody will respect you.
Lao Tzu

Do realize that you have all the answers (to when, what and how to act or think) right here, right now, within you. As you find your way back to yourself (where your belong) you will be able to feel your feelings, express them, and reach for what you need. Those of us who do, whether by early or later learning in life (like right now!), get what we need to be well.

Tune in to your Self. As you learn to slow down, focus on your feelings first, and fascinate over their ebb and flow in any given moment, you are practicing presence. Mindful presence lays in the ability to be in an awe of what is: the silver thread that connects us with each other, and the world, and first, and foremost, with our Selves.

Life gets lonely and hard without an ally, a trustworthy friend who is available when you need him or her. Let me introduce you to your greatest ally in the whole world.

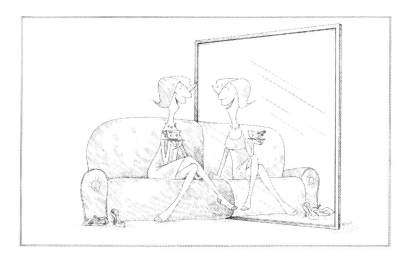

Okay, maybe not yet, because you may not be aware of the hidden gifts this person carries for you. Let's take tally, shall we?

1. You are always there, wherever you are, available to help, guide and soothe;
2. You already know You better than anyone;
3. You already do, or could accept and love you more than anyone;

4. You are all grown up now, and this means you have all the resources you will ever need: focus, wisdom, life experience, intelligence, maturity, willpower, kindness, generosity, words, relationships, information, perseverance, physical strength, and money: all the things you did not have as a child you have now. In fact, chances are you have been utilizing these resources to help others, have you not?
5. You are the only one who has access to how you feel in real time, therefore, you are the one in the best position to help – or ask for it.

Not feeling connected to yourself may give you a sense of uncertainty, a sort of malaise that just lingers on. The antidote is self-love. Practice it, and you find peace, and balance, and joy; top that with good relationships and health. Hard to believe? Learn it here, try it, and you will see. Tapping into your moment-to-moment truth is where the magic of health is galvanized.

Reflection:

- Ask yourself the question: have I been waiting for others or the world to change, and bring me what I need?
- If the answer is yes, repeat this statement to yourself twenty times (you can count on your fingers), and do this twice a day for a week:
  - "I now have what it takes to give myself what I need"
  - "I am taking full responsibility for my life."

Dear One, chances are you could not be in better hands than your own! Think about it...

Your Body, Your Truth

*The intuitive mind is a sacred gift and the rational mind
is a faithful servant. We have created a society that
honors the servant and has forgotten the gift.*
Albert Einstein

Self-love starts with attention to one's Self: this is a *prerequisite* for health, as well as for loving relationships. We can only give to others things that we already possess. This is true not just for material things, but also for certain qualities of relating, like love in its different forms of manifestation: acceptance, kindness, approval, appreciation, attention, and trust.

We can give these to someone else only to the extent we practice them in our relationship to our own Selves. There is one exception, though: our children. Yes, with them, we are often able to overcome our limitations, because we are biologically wired to take care of them and keep them well. Biology, "nature's call" cuts through everything, like a diamond. It over-rules socialization, it always prevails. And *that* is the point: it also prevails over what we *think* is right or wrong to do next, in this very moment.

Intuition lives in our bodies. Let your mind, your reasoning be the humble servant engaged in the service of this vast wisdom that is your body.

This is how Nature guides us:

BODYSENSATION means
FEELING means
NEED means
ACTION

As you perform this action that was derived from the original sensation in your body, you will notice that the sensation diminishes, and that you feel a whole lot better!

Your
ACTION becomes a message from you to your system that you have listened, which makes the
NEED go away, which makes you
FEEL better, which means the uncomfortable
BODY SENSATION is gone, or greatly diminished.

Notice that thought is not involved in this process. Allowing yourself to think while listening to your body would contaminate the process with judgment, or a quick, blanket interpretation. This will short-circuit the body's ability to "talk" and inform you about what the truth of you is in this moment.

Whoever knows himself
Knows God
Muhammad

The body is an artesian well: the information that flows from it is pure and uncontaminated. Nature and humans are one and the same. We are animals – with the added benefit of the ability to reason. Yes, we are creatures made to survive and thrive, and to that end, equipped with everything we need.

Let's take a look at the equipment (don't worry, you are fine, size does not matter here!): your body and your mind are it. Here, on this hemisphere, at this time, we still live under the illusion that our minds alone carry all the answers for peace and happiness. That we can figure out the way to be happy the same way we can figure out math equations. Not so. If we could, we would not be so riddled with mental anguish and physical problems. By the rate we listen to our minds for guidance about how to be well, if it knew, we would all be the picture of inner peace. It does not. Although the mind is smart, it is void of wisdom. It is a sharp, sophisticated tool that serves a purpose: figure out problems, resolve situations with the power of reasoning. Given our relatively frail physical build without this tool we would probably be extinct.

The truth is, health and well-being are not problems - they are a birthright. We are hard-wired to survive and thrive. There is nothing to figure out. The guidance to a happy and healthy life is right here, right now, encoded in our bodies' sensations – and the mind does not have access to that information.

The little flower in the garden does not need much, but what it needs, it MUST HAVE to survive: a lack of safety, water, sunlight, warmth, or nutrients will be the end of its ephemeral, lovely little life. You and I are no different. We have needs, and we will be well in direct proportion to our needs being met – by our own selves, may I add! Needs are by definition non-negotiable. They represent what is fundamentally necessary to survive and thrive, independently from who thinks or wants what. Our thoughts contain our wants. Our bodies carry our needs.

The goal is to be able to access the info on what you need this very moment, and then, the next, to feel better, without interference from anything external – and that includes your own thoughts.

The body's bio-chemistry and the resulting sensations never stop. They speak - in real time - of how we feel. Our feelings and needs are fluid, like the wind or the light, they constantly morph like the waves of energy they are, perpetually seeking the next source of replenishment. Just like animals, we are automatically moved toward what we need, and for the most part, we reach for it without a thought: we breathe, eat, sleep, and procreate. The body – programmed to thrive by Mother Nature - signals these needs through sensations: the discomfort of cravings and irresistible urges. Good! That is why we are still around, despite of our incessant efforts to improve upon perfection.

What we tend to get into trouble with is not so much the foundational needs of food, water, shelter, sex and sleep (not necessarily in that order!). Where we get lost is with our many other needs we actually *can* resist. When we do, we pay a price in the strongest of currencies: health, and happiness.

How about the need for love, acceptance, appreciation, belonging, emotional safety, to name just a few? We have a multitude of needs that fluctuate according to the state of our energetic systems. These are what the Ayurveda, the ancient Indian system of healing calls our many "hungers". You probably know this from looking around you: far too many people do not reach for the things that could quell these hungers. We are held back by guilt, judgment, hopelessness, and shame that our culture instills in us about self-care.

Do you think that paying attention *first and foremost* to your own feelings and needs is stupid, self-centered, selfish or even evil? Join the crowd! Although the bars of social and economic restraints are steadily weakening we still think as people who do not have the freedom to reach for what we need - much like a prisoner set free after a long sentence.

The way to set yourself free, a way that is at your fingertips any given moment is to trust your body! Feel the sensations, let them inform you of the truth of what you need right here and now, and then, and only then, engage your critical thinking, and exclusively to figure out a plan for execution (not to criticize, judge or invalidate in any other way).

This does not mean you must never think - just do not do it instead of feeling!

Follow the healthy order of events. This is even true for people who struggle with addictions, or phobias, or traumas – an interesting topic when it comes to trusting your body, is it not? I will explain my take on this in more detail at the end of Part One. For now, suffice it to say that not even these can adulterate the body's truthful guidance toward health. It is only a matter of knowing how to listen.

Taking It Home:

Put the book down for a moment, and take a deep breath. Feel your body, and answer these questions:

- Do you notice any sensation or urge? Write it down:

  _____

- What is the very first thing you are thinking or telling yourself about this feeling? Write it down (and don't judge yourself!)

  _____

My Thoughtful Reader, your body is the authentic depository of your truths. You are the boss: decide to live according to your truth!

Stress as Information

Health lies at our interface with Nature.
Warren Grossman

Life is stressful, and please do not go thinking that is a bad thing. It is neither bad, nor good, rather, it is necessary. The experience of stress in any and all forms (from hunger, to cold, to tired, to unloved, to worried, etc.) is an expression, as well as a code for an emergent need at the moment. Without stress we would be left uninformed about what we need right here, right now! We can only help what we know about. Stress informs, promptly, and accurately.

It is ingenious in its design, because if it were not uncomfortable, we would not pay attention, now would we? A nice cozy feeling in the belly does not signal hunger, so why go through the trouble of working, shopping for food, and cooking? Alright, maybe you or I would, but that's just because we have plenty of food and some bad habits of eating when not hungry. On a serious note, though, there is no motivation to do anything without discomfort. Even the experience of bursting with energy or love (a good feeling) becomes uncomfortable, if you do not listen to the urge to share it, or if you don't channel it into activity. Thus, discomfort and stress are our greatest – and most truthful - informers about what to do and when. And they live in the body, like every other feeling.

Nature knows best. We have forgotten that we are in good hands with her. Our bodies know and relentlessly communicate through feelings, urges, and physical sensations what we need to do next to be healthy and well. Most of the ones we notice are uncomfortable. Why? Because comfort blends in, feels normal, uneventful. It simply means "stay the course, there is nothing you need to change". Where there is a need for change, there is discomfort. Hunger, cold, loneliness, confusion, any feeling *is* also a stress in the body, which is code for a need, a signal that there is too much, or too little of something - and you must help it.

In our culture we look upon stress and discomfort with suspicion. We somehow made it the enemy, an annoyance to eliminate quickly, rather than embrace and listen to. In our everyday mentality - reflected also in our medical practices - we think of pain and discomfort as abnormal and suspect. This is a huge myth, and an even bigger mistake. In our distrust we ignore or numb our discomfort, physical, or emotional too soon, before it could inform of necessary changes in our lives. Or, we find someone or something to blame for our stress, which distracts us from simply accepting it as the *messenger of the truth.*

My Humble Reader, you can learn to love yourself more by trusting your body's signals. Your whole life will thank you for it - for your whole life!

The Language of the Body

Your intelligence is always with you,
Overseeing your body, even though
You may not be aware of its work.
If you start doing something against
Your health, your intelligence
Will eventually scold you.
Rumi

Nobody knows exactly why it is that bad things happen to good people. Is it fate? Is it luck? Or karma? The answer depends on your persuasion about what makes this world turn. Whatever we think, the fact that whatever happens to us carries a lesson to be learned remains a matter of common observation. In fact, I believe it is all of the above, *and* a mirror for what we need to change in our relationship to our Selves. For how to love ourselves better, how to evolve, and spread the wealth. Everything we think or do, everything that happens to us is a mirror image of our relationship to our Selves: the only thing we can truly help in our lifetime. The body is like a fairy constantly trying to wave and get our attention with its uncanny ability to instantaneously signal imbalance. No filtering, only sensation.

As we pay attention to the physical sensations in our bodies we should be awe-struck by the immediacy of the truths they speak of. This is how it works: the body will first

whisper

its needs, with a little inkling, slight sensation. If you ignore it, it will:

talk louder

with a more distinct sensation. If you are still ignoring it (too busy? distracted? mistrustful?) it will

talk even louder

by way of a discomfort, and if you are *still* absent-minded, it will

yell!

through a pang of pain, and if you are even *still* out to lunch, it will

scream!!

by way of an acute pain, and if you are inattentive to that, then it will bring on some sort of

illness

or

chronic pain

or an

accident

that is hard to ignore, and if you are *still* not getting the point, it will bring on a

disease

or a

catastrophic event

to say "will ya' pay attention already???" By then, you may not even be able to function, so you are effectively stopped in your tracks to - hopefully – wake up, think about what is going on, how you could act, or think, or talk differently, more lovingly, especially toward your own Self? Big words, big meaning: do you pay attention, listen to, communicate with and help your precious Self? Is that your norm?

At this point the question begs itself: what about death? It stands to reason that death also has a place in this string of events: from a far-removed, spiritual perspective we might conceive of death as the "end of the road", the place where our growing into our own Selves, in love and acceptance has reached a dead-end (pun intended), where a new plane of existence is what is necessary for further spiritual evolution. Of course, we all reach that place at one point, even with the best efforts to evolve – that is just a fact of life, and of death.

You might say that things can just happen for no reason, there is something called bad luck, accidents, or flukes. That is certainly true, and the case still remains that it is wise to live with our eyes and minds open to learning from everything that happens, and to take full responsibility for our lives. There is no one to blame, not even yourself; instead of getting hung up on the pain, and the blame, try to make an effort to understand your role in what you are experiencing, so you may learn and grow from it. Everybody gets hurt, and everybody dies, but you have a choice to live your life with less pain and suffering, by striving to be integrated, mature, and aware.

Sally - addicted to painkillers and vastly in denial about it - was only 19 when she suffered a terrible head-on car accident that landed her in the hospital for almost two weeks. She said that the part that bothered her most was not the impact, but the fact, that the other driver did not come to her rescue when she was calling for him. In retrospect she came to realize that the negligent driver was a symbolic representation of her; she was the one who had been absent from herself, not hearing her own cries for a safer, healthier life. The accident woke her up to listen to and take better care of her Self.

The body - or Life - escalates the intensity of our feelings as its ingenious way to get our attention, so that we may take care of our Selves. Now, you can blame all these things on others, or Life, or God, or the Government, and truth be told, that might feel like a relief, temporarily. It always helps to kick the dog, or break a plate, blame someone, or find a scapegoat, but then... nothing really changes, except now you feel even worse, even angrier, more dissatisfied, and guilty.

There is no higher truth than your own feelings, folks, stop looking for it elsewhere! Your doctors, parents, God, therapist, teachers, priests, bosses, psychics, gurus, however well trained and well-meaning, do not know what you need! They may make educated guesses, at best. Only YOU have access to that information, right here, and right now. When you ignore it, things go down in a hand basket. However, when you truly listen inward, and get on board with a healthy direction in your life, all of a sudden everything falls into place, without any effort, right? Bingo!

An unexamined life is not worth living for a human being.

Socrates

If you are still pondering whether you should trust your physical being for guidance in life consider the massive intelligence it takes for the body to repair, replenish, and heal itself day in and day out. Healing comes from within; medicine can only facilitate that healing by optimizing the environment. Which job to take, or what you should have for breakfast – or any other decision for that matter - is a simple task for the body's intelligence, which is capable of the miracle of healing itself.

Reflection:

Are you faced with a decision today? Try this:

- Take a deep breath, unfold your arms, fingers and legs
- Focus on how your body – or any part of it - feels as you think of deciding one way. Does it feel comfortable? Uncomfortable? Does it contract or expand? Is it cold, or warm?
- Take another deep breath, letting that scenario go.
- Think of the other alternative, and notice how your body feels this time

Your authentic decision is the one where your body feels warm, expanded, and relaxed.

Dear Reader, you can shift your attention from "out there" to "in here", from external to internal. You shall be amazed at the steady-handed guidance you will receive – and the ensuing health.

Can I Always Trust My Body?

Many times I have heard the concern: "If I let myself be guided by my body, I will do something bad / against the law / hurtful to others; - I will be selfish and in trouble!" Good thing you brought this up. I would like to ceremoniously beg you to forget this worry. Have some faith in yourself, in knowing right from wrong, will you? Why would you forget the law just because you listen to your body? A silent nod to a need is sometimes all you need to feel better, you don't always have to act on it, especially if it is against your morals. Attention to and acceptance of your feelings is often quite sufficient. No risk of committing something contrary to society's taboos, at least not for most people. Of course, if you have a history of being in trouble with the law or with your conscience, by all means, talk to someone before doing anything hurtful to anyone (including yourself). Allow me to assume, however, this is not *your* case, since you are reading a book on self-evolution and love. No, I am not too worried about you. If anything, you run the risk of having an overgrown conscience, and an overactive mind in need to be quieted a re-focused on the truths within your body.

A lot of people have this worry: if they were to trust their body's signals they would use alcohol, drugs, or do something against the rules of society. No concern is more real than this, but again, do not throw the baby out with the bathwater. Even though the first signal from your body *may* be adulterated by addictions, traumas, or bad behavioral habits the truth about what you really need to be well is still there, imbedded in your body's intelligence.

If you know that you are entangled in unhealthy patterns or illegal habits use your better judgment, despite of what your body might be pulling you to at first. One helpful way to differentiate an adulterated impulse from a healthy instinct is to pay attention to how you feel after the fact: if you feel good, good, if you feel bad, sick, or guilty, it was bad guidance from unhealthy programming. If that is your case, that is not a curse: there is help, and I encourage you to find it!

Sue could tell you many stories the string of bad boyfriends that she just cannot stay away from. They, the bullies, the drunkards and the mean bastards are like a magnet for her, so familiar (her dad was one), yet so destructive in all ways. She says she just cannot help but fall in love with one after the other, only to end up in police stations, hospitals and shelters at the end of each affair. She did not notice that beneath the attraction she had a strong feeling of repulsion as well around men like this. Had she picked up on it, and trusted it, she would have stayed far away from them.

Nix the first impulse if you know it is steering you wrong, and that much you *always* know! Look behind it and ask your body again, for how you feel (you might be surprised by what you find out!) and what you really need to do next to feel better. The information is there, concealed behind the fears and the cravings, because those may be nothing more, but learned programming; there is healthy instinct behind them all, and if you care to look deeper you will find it. When you find it (feelings like hurt, sadness, fear, or anger) accept it with compassion, and let it guide you into the next healthy action (e.g. finding help).

PART TWO

Disconnection

We seldom accept all of ourselves. So many parts are pushed away. When we are feeling frightened, guilty, angry, self-loathing, do we hold ourselves in our arms and cradle ourselves? Do we treat ourselves like our only child? Or do we meet our pain with hatred, rejection, a drowsy blindness that leaves so much of ourselves unexplored and unhealed?

Stephen Levine

The Disconnect Dis-Ease

Your future - whether or not you will be well - is decided in this present moment; it depends on what you do with your feelings, especially your stress. If you let them flood you, if you allow yourself to get lost in them, by despairing or panicking you will end up neglecting to give yourself the necessary help. Under duress you may also be turning on yourself with anger, and meet the initial injury with an insult, self-blame and criticism. Self-abuse is a common reaction to the stress we feel. If and when we meet our pain with lack of care, or blame, the discomfort will turn into suffering, simply because we do not show up in our time of need. The most important trick to creating health and balance is to step out of your feelings of stress and discomfort, while accepting them, and "parent" yourself with them - soothe, approve, love, guide, discipline, etc. This way, you will be okay, and start feeling better.

A friend in need is a friend indeed!
Proverb

The disconnect that causes dis-ease or suffering happens when we abuse or neglect our Selves in the very moment of discomfort or need.

Genetics do play a role in our propensity to certain illnesses, and so does our physical and emotional makeup. Genes are not a curse, they represent only the *potential* for those conditions to develop. Whether or not that potential will actualize itself depends largely on how we treat – i.e. parent - ourselves. Our level of abuse, neglect or love of our Selves (in thought or action) predicts what we create in our relationships and circumstances, and reflects the amount, severity and even types of illnesses and dis-ease we experience in our lives.

Illness is a complex phenomenon; it is neither purely physical, nor purely emotional, nor purely spiritual, but a combination of all three. Dis-ease will manifest on each level of our existence. A stomach ache is also emotional unease. Sadness manifests as a heaviness in the heart as well.

We often deny this complexity by reacting – as opposed to responding - to the stress we feel. It is easy to brush it off by saying "it's only because .....", or to quell it with a pill. Instead of allowing it to speak to us, and then soothing ourselves so we may hear its message, we get stuck with it by either shutting it down or over-reacting to it. Paradoxically, this clinging, this getting stuck to the pain by not distancing and taking care is the way we disconnect from our truth. The mind is not listening to the body, and the guidance is lost on us. The Buddha called this suffering, the attachment on the most fundamental level, to our own pain.

Now, you must not worry about not noticing when you are disconnected – either temporarily or chronically – from your feelings. Nature will give us feedback, makes sure that we take notice, by hitting us with ever escalating discomfort – until we do take notice. Disconnect, or lack of acknowledgment of our feelings and lack of adequate self-care leads to dis-ease, which leads to illness. Each and every emotional illness represents a certain degree of disconnect from one's Self; the greater the disconnect between the body's messages and the mind's ability to read them as such, the more severe the mental or emotional disorder. Here is a partial rundown on what some of the symptoms of such disconnect may be:

Emotional problems: feeling depressed, anxious, angry, overwhelmed, tired/exhausted, unmotivated, unfocused, sad, angry, burnt out; in extreme cases losing time, or having a psychotic break. You will find more information on depression as you read on.

<u>Addictions:</u> to any substance, including alcohol, drugs, cigarettes, chocolate, soda, and even food; to any activity, including gambling, shopping, exercising, hoarding, promiscuity, philandering, using porn, overworking, or being obsessive about anything in thought or behavior.

<u>Relationship Problems:</u> aggression or absence, that is abuse or neglect in any relationship (including toward yourself) leads to divorce, inability to find a partner, parent/child conflicts, workplace conflicts, unsatisfactory friendships, or a recurrent pattern of troubled, unstable, volatile or distant relationships.

<u>Health Problems</u>: whether chronic or acute, they are signs of some level of disconnect, or internal conflict. Our immunity, the body's energetic balance is dependent upon it getting what it needs. Illnesses develop as a result of unmet physical or emotional needs, as the body manifests the misalignment between feelings and thoughts (or body and mind, or heart and reasoning). They are also a way of the body trying to get our attention by intensifying and escalating the discomfort.

<u>Aches and Pains:</u> Each body part tells the story of some type of disconnect or lack of self-care. Think how worrying causes headaches, fear manifests neck and shoulder pains, stress leads to digestive problems, and the way grief is connected with the heart. Check out Louise Hay's book "You Can Heal Your Life", where she elaborates on the meaning of symptoms in different parts of the body.

<u>Accident-proneness:</u> A pattern of getting into small or big accidents for no apparent reason is very often due to a lack of acknowledgment – i.e. abuse or neglect – of one's feelings (e.g. tiredness, sadness, anger, etc.). The function of accident-proneness is to get others' attention and care. In the case of children it is a sign that his feelings or needs are being ignored.

Why Do We Disconnect?

The drive to connect with one's Self is profound and eternal, albeit not always possible. In the developed world we are living a veritable historic first, because a majority of us have the luxury to be authentic, to reach for personal happiness. This is not something most people can afford in many other parts of the world, where poverty, oppression, tradition, religion, dogma, or custom keep people living oppressed, in the bondage of disconnect, and inauthenticity. Unlike in a democratic society, where the law provides - if imperfect - protection for self-determination and individual freedoms, in more traditional societies it is often unwise, if not outright dangerous to profess and act on one's desires. Also, many people have no choice but to live in conflict with themselves, a schizoid state where their convictions (cultural, religious, or political ideas and thoughts) are in direct contradiction with their human conscience or nature (love of self and others). This internal split is tremendously stressful; obviously, not good for health or longevity.

I have spoken to many people who would love to be able to feel their feelings and express them, except, they are paralyzed by fear. Fear of being seen and heard is a common outcome of childhood neglect or abuse. If a child is punished, or ignored for hurting (e.g. crying, complaining, and asking for help) he will learn either to not feel or to not talk. He will also become generally depressed or angry, because human beings cannot be well without sharing, in emotional isolation from others. We need each other to be healthy, and needs, again, are by definition non-negotiable.

Although it comes from ancient programming, the fear of being "out there", visible and audible must be dissolved. As an adult, you have nothing to fear; worst case scenario you will be ignored or blamed, right? Guess what, you now have what it takes to stick up for yourself, and to surround yourself with people who are willing and able to share with you. Do this, and *let the chips fall where they may*. You will not be alone. You will actually clear some space in your life for the right kind of people to come in: loving, accepting, positive. As you make emotional and physical room in your life, they will appear, I promise!

Very often people ignore their internal conflicts because they think this means they have to quit, cut someone off, or make some other life-altering decision. That is pretty scary; hey, who wants to overhaul their lives just like that? But don't worry: in most instances, accepting the truth of how you feel will enable you to negotiate a different arrangement *within* your existing job, relationship or any other situation. In other words, it will allow you to assert yourself. You do not have to throw the baby out with the bathwater, you can have what and whom you want, and make it suit your needs better! If – God forbid - it does not work, after you trying in different ways, you can always reconsider whether or not you actually need that relationship, job, or situation in your life.

Do you think you cannot or will not be heard? Think again. Could it be that thus far it did not happen because you did not speak in a way that *could* be heard? Were you perhaps either too silent, or too loud to be heard? Passive, or aggressive? That is not assertive. Assertive is the only style of communication with the power to negotiate the best possible deal for everyone involved. It is a skill that can be learned. You can learn it here and now (under Third Step, Assertiveness in Part Five) - and let the negotiations begin!

Dearest, stop shrinking yourself, choose YOU, make yourself visible and audible; everything else will take care of itself.

The Shabby Childhood

There was a bumper sticker in the 80's that said "A nuclear bomb can ruin your whole day". Soon, a postcard followed, saying "A nuclear family can ruin your whole life". Do not buy it, it is not true. Sure, it can temporarily ruin one's faith and courage in life. It can drain one's personal sense of empowerment and entitlement to build a good life. It can disconnect your mind from your body. A shabby childhood will indeed serve up a hefty dose of bad programming, but it is only that: learning. What you can learn, you can un-learn and re-learn.

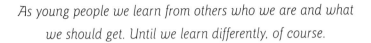

As young people we learn from others who we are and what we should get. Until we learn differently, of course.

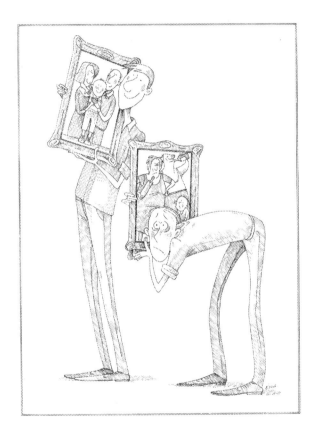

Don't think you are alone if you feel your childhood was not the greatest. There have always been sick, dysfunctional families, riddled with mental illness, addictions and violence. In these extreme cases, children are given a sad legacy of trauma, and the resulting coping mechanisms that will need to be rewritten throughout their whole lives to find safety and peace of mind. Throughout history parenting practices we would consider bad today were the norm however - even without illness in the family. Until very recently, in fact all the way into the eighties, when the child abuse reports started coming out, it was common perception among parents, educators, and other "trendsetters" in our society that children are to be seen and not heard. Punished, and not cuddled. Shamed, and not praised. Made to feel guilty, and not appreciated. Humbled, and not elevated (God forbid, they would be proud!) Criticized, and not encouraged. Ignored, and left alone.

Possibly, some of this was well-intended. It was based partially on material necessity, as well as on age-old cultural and religious teachings, the persuasion that positive feedback would spoil a child, while negative feedback would prod him or her to do better. Very understandably, the way children took it, for the most part, is that they should not do better, but be better; that there is something wrong with them; that they are somehow not good enough.

Any pattern of negative feedback, whether through put-downs, criticism, physical punishment, i.e. abuse, or neglect translates into feelings of inadequacy, low self-esteem and weakened confidence. To top this joyous scenario, the pain that this type of parenting causes makes kids want to disconnect from that experience – and they do! In order to protect themselves, children get lost in their imagination to escape, or in their thoughts, in a frantic attempt to figure out a way to help themselves or prevent trouble. They may become anxious, depressed, and hyper-vigilant. All that time spent "up there" in the mind creates a pattern of disconnect from experiencing the present moment: a very helpful tool, indeed, to stay as intact as possible in the midst of suffering. This is the main reason why some people do not have any memory of their childhood years: you cannot recall experiences that you did not register in the first place!

As that child grows up he will still be disconnected from his body, and have a hard time being present. What was most helpful then becomes the greatest hurdle, because the body's signals are the very source of vital information about how to be well. This is when a person must re-learn how to be present, and live in their body.

An abusive or neglectful upbringing can be a trap because as we grow up we will use what we have, the same methods for treating ourselves as the ones we received earlier from others. People who were physically or emotionally, or even sexually abused, will do the same in adulthood: aggress on their own – and others' - feelings and/or body, and, by extension, allow others to do the same to them. Same goes for neglect: those of us who were physically or emotionally neglected, will do just that as adults: not pay attention to our own feelings and needs, or even bodies, and, by extension, let others do the same to us.

There you have it: the bucket gets passed down the generations, the cycle of abuse and neglect continues - until someone questions it, and learns how to stop it. You are now holding the instructions in your hand. What type of parenting did you grow up with? If you don't remember, just take an honest look at how you treat yourself today.

Tomorrow, my Dear, is a new day, and you are FREE to change the patterns that hurt you in the past. *Like:*

Abuse and Neglect: The Evil Twins

The Evil Twins roam the world causing pain and suffering wherever they rear their ugly heads; sometimes they are easily recognizable, but often they use a mask. Their smartest, most undetectable disguise is when they live inside of us, and make us mistreat ourselves, using our minds to justify their actions.

Would you agree that they are the worst of enemies? *Really?* You see, historically, these ways of relating did not used to be looked down on, quite the contrary! Even just a couple of generations ago good, loving, intelligent people were told that when the child is misbehaving, a good parent should blame, shame or even hit him. These "parenting tools" were deemed wholesome and helpful, ones apt to teach a child how to adapt in this world. Then again, the world was a very cruel place, pretty much everywhere. Children truly had to be taught to ignore their feelings and submit to any authority, even if tyrannical, because that *was* the reality they had to live and survive in. Abusive and neglectful parenting practices in some ways actually prepared children to adapt and survive in an abusive and neglectful society.

On the pedagogical side the thinking was that these techniques will train the child to withstand pain, and motivate him to avoid mistakes in the future, by virtue of developing aversion to the consequences. There is a saying in my native Hungarian that goes something like "the palm tree grows under a weight", meaning, give them hardship to help them to thrive. (Do people really put a weight on young palm trees, I wonder?) Along the lines of what does not kill you makes you stronger, I guess. So this part takes care of the abuse as a recommended way to raise children. It gets better: historically, parenting practices also involved leaving them alone (i.e. not playing, or even talking with a child other than ordering him around), so they will learn to occupy themselves; not soothe them so they learn to soothe themselves; and not giving them too much attention, so they learn they are not "the center of the universe". You guessed, the word is neglect. It wasn't until the French enlightenment, in the 18th Century that children's innate goodness and right to be treated with respect and care was even formulated (by Jean Jacques Rousseau, in his book "Emile, or On Education"). Of course, these ideals took a couple of centuries to seep into our parenting practices. In the 1950's abuse and neglect were still the predominant – and widely recommended - styles of parenting.

"Everything is good as it leaves the hands of the Author of
things; everything degenerates in the hands of man."
Jean-Jacques Rousseau

Is any of this familiar to you? Because if it is, you have had some experiences of feeling abused (physically, emotionally, verbally or sexually), or neglected (physically or emotionally) yourself. Hurt is hurt, no one ever got healthier or better because of it. It only generates more of itself. Hurt people hurt people, as the saying goes. What goes around, comes around.

If you want your finances, car, garden, job, your *anything* to do well, you put positive attention and care into it, right? The same is true for people - and that includes you, in relationship to yourself. Any relationship will suffer from any shade of abuse or neglect; avoid them like the plague.

If you really want to be well give yourself attention (the opposite of neglect) and care (the opposite to abuse) – and thrive you will!

Socialization

The hardest challenge is to be yourself in a world where
everyone is trying to make you be somebody else.
E .E. Cummings

Through our history and socialization we have learned not to listen to our stress. We have made virtue out of the necessity to ignore our feelings, and carry on. This is something our ancestors *had to do* to cope with the harshness of their reality. For most people in the world throughout human history there was no such thing as the luxury to expect feeling good, being healthy, let alone happy. It is still a luxury in most places. In the Western world however, for the first time ever in our evolution we now have the science and guidance to actually reach for personal health and happiness (these two are synonyms!) on a mass scale. How? Rather paradoxically, by learning to listen, accept, and decode the stress our bodies carry.

What is wrong with us, anyway, with being just the way we are? What is wrong with expressing ourselves, being honest, just straight up open and clear about our preferences? Why do we hide the truth and live our lives pretending?

As discussed earlier, the reasons are historic, cultural and religious, and altogether formidable. Every step of the way in our upbringing and socialization we are taught to ignore our feelings and to do what we are told. We "get the message" not only through verbal teachings, but also attitudes, actions, guilt, shaming, in all of their spectacular hues of the rainbow. When family and society do not offer help and comfort at our time of need we are shown through the power of neglect how feelings don't matter. No wonder so many people numb or do not trust their feelings - and have long forgotten what they are missing.

> *Even subtle messages can be very powerful in their impact about life lessons. When I was around five one day in daycare we were set to go to the playground, and the teacher was holding a very appealing ball in her hands, looking around for who should be the lucky kid to carry the ball – a great privilege! The kids went crazy, jumping and yelling "Me! Me!!!" The air was thick with suspense - but, for some odd reason I was not interested in the task. And then it happened: the teacher handed the ball to me, saying that I deserved it, given that I did not act out in excitement, like everybody else. HELLO! I was NOT interested! We all learned an important lesson that day: to not want, or to not reach for what we want – and, that life is not fair!*

Thus, the Evil Twins, are not the only culprits for misery in the world. Culture is doing the lion's share of invalidating people's feelings and needs. Some of it seems to come from distorted cultural and religious precepts that make us feel selfish, guilty or ashamed if we pay attention to our own needs. Jesus said "Love thy neighbor as you love thyself", meaning you must love yourself first and then be as kind to others as you are to yourself. Where is the part where you must loathe, diminish, and otherwise dismiss yourself? It is like the game of telephone: by the time you get to the end of the line, the message becomes unintelligible.

Humankind's history had been riddled all along by poverty, wars, epidemics, i.e. life or death struggles, and so - in the interest of the survival of the collective - people had to pull together and set their individual needs aside.

I have recently read my family's history in the recollection of my great-aunt Borishka. In it she says that in our family all the way up until the 1920's the pronoun "I" was not in use; only "we" existed, as in "We think that...", "We don't do that".

We have inherited a culture where the messages we receive from parents, teachers, preachers and other authority figures are all in cahoots about what is good and right - and to a great extent they tend to invalidate the individual's own feelings and needs.

Paralyzing Messages

The following are some of the messages many of us received growing up:

"Idle hands are the playthings of the Devil" -
"Don't just sit there, do something!"
"Don't be selfish (lazy, stupid)"
"It is selfish of you to want that"

"Use your head"

"You are not the center of the Universe"

"You are the patient, I am the doctor"

"Me, me, me!"

"Children are to be seen and not to be heard"

"Do what I say, not what I do"

"Do what you are told!"

"Be humble"

"You are on your own!"

"Who do you think you are?"

"You are no better than anyone else!"

"Don't be prideful (arrogant, disrespectful, conceited)!"

"Don't toot your own horn!"

"Spare the rod, spoil the child!"

"Do what I say, not what I do!"

Can you remember what messages you grew up with? If so, fill in the blank below with them; it helps to be acutely aware of the old "rules" that might still steer you away from being – and loving – your true Self:

_____

_____

While the times those messages were helpful have passed, here we are, stuck with a pervasive pattern of disconnect from our feelings and needs.

> *I once knew a very bright and accomplished man, I'll call him Joe; he had been depressed all his life, because he never wanted to break his family's rules, or be bad, or become a "narcissist" or "selfish" by allowing himself to be happy and proud of who he was. Needless to say, people around him were none the happier for his sacrifice! In fact, he was so miserable they had to constantly take care of him.*

We must not forget, however that these old directives were helpful and necessary at the period in history when they were born. They were "coping mechanisms" on a social scale. The thing with coping mechanisms is that with the situation changing they lose their adaptive power, and they become not only obsolete, but even a hindrance. That is our cue that it is time to find new rules to live by! Rules that are positive, validating, kind and inclusive. Rules that empower you and me to appreciate who we are, and to feel good about ourselves. Ones that enable us to trust ourselves. Why? Because it is what is healthy, and because now we *can*.

> *Earl, son of a minister was shaking as he told me about how he felt all his life: "I always thought the only way to avoid thinking that I am the center of the Universe is by saying bad things to myself about myself. I was taught that if I think good thoughts of myself I am doing something immoral, making myself into a false idol."*

I believe in a way we are all idols. Real, not false. We are sacred carriers of truths, qualities, and talents this world needs: walking and breathing archetypes. Deep inside we all carry all the wisdom and greatness of the whole, just as a single drop carries all the components of the ocean itself. I suspect it is now mostly by force of habit that we are making virtue out of squeezing ourselves into square boxes, and continue pushing ourselves down.

One of the more subtle messages we all receive is that there is something wrong with our preferences (other than as consumers of goods). To be told that you are selfish (or wrong) for wanting what you want. The truth is, preferences are feelings, and feelings are born out of needs, and we always have them, right or wrong, no matter who thinks what – including our own Selves. From this angle, judging preferences, is somewhere between nonsense and emotional abuse.

> *There is nothing wrong with your preferences,*
> *as long as nobody is getting hurt.*

Nobody's preferences are "truer" or "more right" than others'. They are just a thing of nature, and they must be accepted, expressed, and then negotiated with the preferences of others.

Our differences in likes and preferences are as normal as people living in different bodies. They are dictated by our momentary and ever-changing physical and emotional needs. Honoring preferences is basic respect for one's Self and for others.

Society's zeal to erase individual preferences comes, again, from a valid place: history. Pretty much all of humankind's social and economic evolution, whereby, for the majority of people there was a constant shortage in resources, such as food, safety, hygiene, education, while social, political, and familial structures were riddled with tyranny, oppression and exploitation. (Sadly, this is still the case in many parts of the world today.)

The survival of the family and the interests of the collective overruled any notion of individual freedom, and the community often ruthlessly snuffed such attempts. Throughout our history everyone was a slave to the mores of the times, and the rules of conduct imposed by the current secular and religious authorities. "Be yourself" was never a message for the individual Paul or Mary to live by.

This is largely so even to this day – with one, rather palpable difference: in our industrialized era we have the *resources* necessary for individual happiness, self-realization and thriving on a massive scale. Most people have access to the necessary information and guidance, and families, as well as communities have somewhat loosened their grip on what people do with their lives.

Of course, we *are* collective beings; you might have noticed that *what is truly healthy and good for one person is truly healthy and good for everyone else around them.*

Therefore, do not worry about listening to your truth, because it is saturated with intelligence and life-enhancing vitamins for everyone. Just as long as the choices come from within each one of us, we can spread the wealth outward – but not the other way around.

In the past five, or more millennia very few had the luxury to listen to their individual inklings. Juxtapose that with your tall, skim, two shot decaf latte with whip. Our world is sure changing; it is now time to expand our freedom as consumers into the realm of the Self, where the potential for true happiness lies.

Socialization happens by incessant learning, and the learning never stops. What we can learn we can unlearn by practicing new patterns of behavior, thinking and feeling. We now get to break the mold and reach for more than just survival: for thriving - both physically and emotionally!

You see, there is hope yet. You are living in the first time in history when for most people in the Western world personal happiness is more than just a pipe dream; it is a practical reality that you can reach for by simply making peace with your own feelings; health, good relationships, peace and joy sprout automatically from that practice. In the chapter Your Steps to Self-Love you can learn how.

Dear _____ (your name),
EXPAND. BREATHE. FEEL. TRUST.

Feeling Selfish?

Don't give up on your own welfare
For the sake of others' welfare, however great.
Clearly know your own welfare
And be intent on the highest good.
The Dhammapada

Self-centered is the only perspective we have in life. It is not a moral issue, it is just the way we are built. No one can see the world through someone else's eyes, wishes, desires, or fears. We only have one perspective: our own. We live in separate bodies, and they are hard-wired for feeling, knowing what is healthy. Feelings, needs and preferences are messengers of our own truths at any given moment in time. Truth is truth, it doesn't get any purer than that!

There is only *my* truth (feeling, need, preference), and *your* truth (feeling, need, preference), no other Truth is manifested anywhere in the universe. Others' preference is not truer than yours. At the point where two preferences collide there is communication: you can and must explain, and educate the other about your needs, and then negotiate plans of action that honor both parties' preferences. The result is a caring resolution to the satisfaction of all parties involved. Whenever this process is stunted there is a risk of selfish behaviors.

Our heads are filled with misguided notions about who we are and what we must do in this life. People who take advantage of others are labeled as selfish (and rightly so), while others, who just have a plain preference are also labeled as selfish (wrongly so). Many people grow up thinking we must exploit ourselves on the job, at home and in the community to be thought of well. In prevalently protestant cultures – like in the United States - time off, breaks, vacations, idling around, creative activities, along with playtime and intimacy are deemed unproductive, thus generating guilt in those who even ponder such things. We end up feeling exhausted, sick and tired, because we abuse and neglect our own Selves as a way of life, in order to avoid feeling – or being labeled as – selfish.

If you feel like a bad person for wanting to be well, stop. It is your birthright, in fact, your main mandate. Selfish behavior is quite the opposite of self-care. It is a result of not getting your needs met, and then proceeding to reach for something you do not really need. Choosing your own convenience over someone else's true needs is selfish. But do not confuse convenience with necessity. Choosing what is necessary for your wellbeing over someone else's preferences is not only not selfish, it is self-care. That self-care is a pre-requisite for generosity is a truth that only seems paradoxical on the surface.

The main reason for a pattern of selfish behavior is stunted growth: in lack of adequate nutrients any living organism would be desperately reaching for more, driven and absorbed by the hungry Self. In a human being when some fundamental needs are not met during the early years maturation is stunted, and the person is "stuck". Only when you get what you need can you fully mature, and then be altruistic, by giving from the overflow. Hence, it is normal for children and adolescents to behave in a selfish way. They are still in the process of growing in self-awareness that is knowing their truth: how they feel and what they need to feel better. Moreover, they do not yet have the skills and tools to meet their needs. A larger awareness follows from self-awareness, just like altruism springs forth from self-care.

Examples of selfish behaviors include blaming or criticizing others for asking for what they need, or ignoring others' needs. This is born from blaming, criticizing or ignoring one's Self in a time of need. Deep down the culprit for selfish behaviors is lack of adequate attention, or compassion to one's own feelings and needs.

It stands to reason that the only stance that is decent and fair to your Self, as well as to others is to care.

Compassionate toward yourself
You reconcile all beings in the world.
Lao Tzu

When you don't get what you need there will be an imbalance, a dis-ease, and you will burden others, having to rely on them to do *your* job, and compensate for what you lack in. If it is necessary, sure, do rely, we all need help when we are sick or down. Is it necessary though for you to be weakened or down if you could help it by simply paying attention to your needs and meeting them? By loving yourself? How can others love you more than you do yourself – and why should *they* do what only you can? It is actually selfish to *not* put yourself first, don't you agree?

Loving yourself...does not mean being self-absorbed or narcissistic,
or disregarding others. Rather, it means welcoming
yourself as the most honored guest in your own heart,
a guest worthy of respect, a lovable companion.
Margo Anand

You cannot overdo fulfilling a need, simply because once it is met it will cease to be. Therefore, you cannot be selfish by reaching for *all* that you need. But if you don't, you will end up hungry, which is a setup for reaching for a substitute, something you don't really need, or not as much of it: a temporary fix, a substitute like money, drugs, alcohol, position, power. Not that there is anything wrong with money, or a drink, or power, or position: it is only when people reach for these things *as substitutes* that they become selfish, hurtful to others. This is a direct outcome of self-abuse, or self-neglect when feeling uncomfortable.

"My mission in life is not merely to survive, but to thrive;
and to do so with some passion, some compassion,
some humor, and some style"

Maya Angelou

You can only be good to the extent you are well. Health is positive energy. When you are sick, or tired, you are deficient in positive energy. No one can give from an empty satchel. The more you give yourself the things you really need, like love, acceptance, attention, soothing, communication, and the such, the better you feel, and the more of it you can give to others. Relating positively to others happens simply by extension, by virtue of you practicing these qualities in your relationship to yourself.

Most people have a modicum of guilt or discomfort thinking of themselves first. We still do at times, but we try to hide it, or cover it up with a white lie as if there was something wrong with it. "Sorry, I can't come to the party, I have work to do" (really?), or "Yes, I would be happy to do that" (not!). Saying yes to others is often a lie toward one's Self; we betray ourselves by saying "come on, you can do it, don't be selfish, you are not that tired, this is more important", etc.

Do you realize what damage this causes inside of you? How much energy you "bleed" in the process? It causes serious internal conflict, and then perpetuates it, by extension, between you and others. This is when the enemy is within the doors: *as we focus on external expectations rather than on internal whispers and urges we lose track of our own truth.*

This is also how we lose faith in ourselves, in our ability to reach for what we need, and feel peaceful, well, lovable and important. Living in denial of how we truly feel causes an internal war that is exhausting, and depressing. It drains our sense of self-empowerment, simply because there is literally no one "home" you could trust. No one to bring your pain to, who would listen, accept and help. Truth is, *you* are the one who must and can be that person in the first place. When you do that, others follow suit. When you do not, others don't either. Call it selfish, call it whatever you will, the fact remains, you are the one Nature put in charge of you.

It is time you afford the luxury of giving yourself the compassion you deserve. Compassion is being positive, validating, loving, caring, and present. It is the way you want to be in this world. If this makes you feel selfish, then you can do this with good conscience for the sake of others! Giving more to others than to yourself is not sustainable: you will find yourself becoming an empty mask, faking more joy and love than what you really have. You cannot give from an empty container without feeling depleted and resentful. Instead, fill your own container first, and then give to others from the overflow. Don't buy into the destructive myth that this is selfish.

Our entire life... consists ultimately in
accepting ourselves as we are.
Jean Anouilh

An important consideration: when you find yourself thinking of someone in your surroundings as selfish ask yourself before you get deeper into judgment, have I made it clear what I need from this person? Have I been assertive, that is positive and specific regarding my expectations, and did I really mean it?

I often find that people label each other when they are disappointed. If this is you, consider this your chance to take care of yourself by taking responsibility for getting your needs met. We shall delve deeper into the how-am-I-gonna-do-that part, in the chapter on Assertiveness.

> *Dearest, you are good enough just the way you are. If you notice*
> *you give too much, or too little to others it is because you are*
> *not getting what you need. When you make sure you do, your*
> *life will rebalance itself and you will give from the overflow.*

Pain and Discomfort

And could you keep your heart in wonder at the daily miracles of
your life, your pain would not seem less wondrous than your joy;
And you would accept the seasons of your heart, even as you
have always accepted the seasons that pass over your fields.
And you would watch with serenity
Through the winters of your grief.
Kahlil Gibran

In our culture pain is vilified, while pleasure is fetishized. This is a forced dichotomy; truth is, pain and joy dwell in one and the same space. To unlock one is to free the other. You are either open or closed. Open happens to be conducive to health, while closed is a highway to disease.

Men are born soft and supple;
Dead, they are stiff and hard.
Plants are born tender and pliant;
Dead, they are brittle and dry.

Thus whoever is stiff and inflexible
Is a disciple of death.
Whoever is soft and yielding
Is a disciple of life.
Lao Tzu

Whether we yield or resist, are soft or stiff is a matter of our own choice. *On a fundamental level it is probably the only thing we truly have a choice over in life. Go with, or go against. Be with, or resist.*

Being the ingenious surviving machine it is the body *always* senses, moment to moment, day and night. It senses, and it feels both comfort and discomfort. Sensation is our greatest ally in survival and thriving – in fact, the more intense the sensation (e.g. pain, or a burst of energy), the more informative, the more important it is for our well-being.

Take pain, for instance. In therapy circles PAIN spells "Pay Attention Inside Now!" If you do that, you will fare just fine. For the most part however we graduate childhood having learned that pain is abnormal, a problem that must be quickly done away with. Our whole medical philosophy is geared toward alleviating pain and suffering. There is nothing wrong with that, except often this is done too soon, *before* it could inform us of underlying patterns in the relationship to Self. In our haste we are throwing the baby out with the bathwater: the information that the pain is designed to deliver in the first place, the one without which we cannot be well.

Do not curse your discomfort, physical or emotional, because it is *not* a sign of illness - it is a sign that you are healthy. *Do not look upon pain and discomfort as your enemy, or kill the messenger who just came to bring you news you literally cannot live without.*

Your system is simply stepping in and alerting you that something is wrong, and you must correct it, by addressing how you treat yourself when you feel uncomfortable. You know, like when you get the flu, and deep down you have a strong sense that you needed to rest anyway, you just did not listen?

Illness, my friend, is designed to keep us well in two ways: by localizing the problem into one area or function of the body, thus preventing it from becoming systemic and pervasive, and also by informing us about what needs to happen to be well. Don't give yourself any guilt or reprimands when you are sick, though: that would be another distraction from positive action, and another drain on your energy.

Being a signaling mechanism symptoms are never superfluous. Stay connected to your pain or discomfort, so they may inform you – unless there is absolutely nothing more you can do about them – and even then, you must stay present to feel your powerlessness and grieve your loss.

Let us tally some examples of discomfort or pain we may habitually ignore, or chalk up to some "condition", thus avoiding taking responsibility for making changes. You may want to check the ones that apply to you:

- Chronic fatigue
- Irregular breath
- Ache in the heart area
- Stomach pain, discomfort
- Pressure in the chest area
- Jaw clenching
- Dry mouth

- ▫ Lump in the throat
- ▫ Heaviness in limbs
- ▫ Dizziness
- ▫ Muscle tension
- ▫ Back pain
- ▫ Shoulder pain
- ▫ Nervousness
- ▫ Irritability
- ▫ Ticks
- ▫ Sleep problems (too much, too little, or disturbed)
- ▫ Nightmares
- ▫ No appetite
- ▫ Overeating
- ▫ Cravings (for alcohol, drugs, or other means of escape)

If you checked any of the above, do see a doctor. If you are found to be in good health, take a deep breath, and smile: you are not on "Candid Camera", but you are being alerted, gifted with vital information about the fact that there is something you must do, or stop doing, so you may feel better. Now you are listening!

Symptoms are good attention-getters, but noticing is just a portal to understanding the message. In the chapter Your Steps to Self-Parenting with Love you will learn how to translate this information into positive, life changing actions. Excited? Good!

You can only help what you know about. Deeper inquiry into your discomfort will do a lot of good (so stop thinking of it as a pain in the neck!). It will:

- Inform you of how you actually feel;
- Inform you of what you need to do, or say, or be like *right now* to feel better;

- Save you from further discomfort, because you will lower it by listening and making sure you get what you need;
- Save you from the discomfort possibly escalating into illness;
- Establish a pattern of self-acceptance and self-care that will enhance your health in the future, and minimize the recurrence of the same symptoms.

Physicians diagnose from our symptoms, and diagnoses are limited to the physical plane. Not even doctors have access to the wisdom of each person's body, and to what *exactly* that symptom is trying to communicate. Thus, medicine targets the symptom, but not the underlying patterns, the part, and not the whole, the physical, and not the energetic. From this perspective medicine is limited by its own tools.

Medical science is highly effective in treating our ailments, but not in healing them. Healing comes from the body, it is in the information behind the symptoms, pointing to physical/emotional/spiritual patterns in one's relationship to one's Self. *Body, mind, spirit, emotions are all different manifestations of one and the same system.* They are not separate entities, but more like members of a family. When you are not feeling well, they may act out like kids in a household.

What determines the patterns in our systems? Although history, genes, and legacies all play a role, *we humans are ultimately free in choosing the level to which we give ourselves permission to be well.* Ironically, that level will match the one to which we allow ourselves to feel discomfort. Either we feel, or we do not. This is a loaded reality: it implies *choosing* to feel, to connect within, and then aligning our thoughts, and actions with that choice. It's what I call a life's work.

Just remember: pain and discomfort are messengers
of how well you love yourself. Use them to motivate
you to pay attention and correct your ways.

Necessary Pain – Tolerate It!

Disappointment, defeat, and despair
are the tools God uses to show us the way.
Paulo Coelho

Any and all feeling or sensation you have is by definition necessary. If it was not, you would not have it. The source, or cause of stressful sensations, however can be either necessary or unnecessary.

Mind you, most of the things that cause us discomfort are a normal part of life: you get hungry, traffic is a pain, too much to do. Growing pains are necessary. Birthing pain is necessary, and so is the one we feel when we grieve, and also when we lose something, like a job, a house, a valuable object, an opportunity, health, or youth.

Change is stressful, at times even painful. The physical and emotional discomfort is a necessary component of healing, regrouping and growing. Without the discomfort we would not do what is necessary to adjust, adapt, stay alive and thrive. If nothing else, on the physical level when a loved one dies or leaves us we must cry in order to get rid of the toxins the stress causes in the body.

When a woman delivers a child the pain is designed to urge her to push with all her might when the time is ripe. When we cut our leg, and it bleeds, the pain alerts us to pay attention and tend to the wound: without it we may get infected, or even bleed to death.

Conflict with others is also unavoidable, thus necessary. Don't panic! We are all different, with ever-changing preferences, of course they have to be explained, matched up and negotiated! Stay, calm down, talk, resolve. With normal, necessary pain this is usually a process that you must be able to stay with. Tolerate the discomfort long enough to let it guide you toward healing.

Necessary pain and discomfort are our greatest allies in life, our motivators and body-guards, true life-savers. Feeling uncomfortable informs us about when and what to do to be well.

So, as you learn to pay attention to the sensations in your body *you are increasing your threshold of tolerance for discomfort.* Instead of *reacting* to the discomfort by shutting down (flight reaction), or judging it or yourself (fight reaction), you are being responsive (you will find more on this in the chapter on Reactivity). Instead of running away from it, cutting it short, and in general treating it as your enemy, you will soothe yourself into allowing it to be there. You will learn to breathe, and linger with the discomfort *just long enough* for it to fulfill its function: to inform you regarding your next best move, decision, word, or action. *Therefore, the goal is not to get over the pain, but to get into it!*

Shunning necessary pain is tantamount to a disastrous life. Do not numb your discomfort with drugs, alcohol, frantic activity, shopping, gambling, TV, food, over-working, socializing, or any other means of distraction! These will temporarily distract you from the way you are feeling, but will eventually add to the list of what needs to be tended to. If any of these becomes an addiction, and it will if you are using it to numb pain, then you will face two problems, instead of one.

If you are numbing your feelings, STOP and FEEL! This will not make it worse: you are just going to *actually experience* the truth of how you are feeling. You can learn to *tolerate* normal discomfort and pain; but you do not have to tolerate it forever, just long enough to be able to read it for its information value - and then quickly do what you found out. That is when the discomfort will cease, and be truly resolved. It will simply fulfill its function of getting your attention and informing you. Isn't that what your daily newspaper does? This is a matter of learning to read your body to get the 411 on *the* most vital and relevant information of the day, month, year, or maybe your entire life. Don't skip it! Become a lifetime subscriber!

Sometime during our growing up years, we learn through experience and socialization that pleasure is good and pain is bad. As we come of age we realize that pain can be really helpful. Solitude, sorrow, crying, soul-searching in our hour of angst can be just what the doctor ordered to reclaim peace and balance in our lives.

Reflection:

Is your tolerance for necessary pain too low? Tweak it up! In the Appendix you will find the exercise Your Baseline of Unhappiness that can help with this.

Who or what, My Dear is in the way of you taking care of yourself – especially when feeling down or hurt? If you really think about it, only you can stop you from being well. Stop that stopping!

Unnecessary Pain (or Suffering) – Do Not Tolerate It!

Any hurt that you can help is by definition unnecessary. The pain and discomfort that come from feeling mistreated must be used as energy and motivation to change the situation. This type of pain can come from basically two sources: you and the people around you. You have the power – indeed, the obligation! - to stop both.

When we live in a situation that is not healthy the physical or emotional pain is there to nudge and urge us to pay attention and make changes: without it we would do nothing, change nothing – and get sick, or even die. If there is abuse or neglect present in your life circumstances trust your gut feelings: they will push you to do something to challenge it, and hopefully, change it. If this is not possible, the only way to be well is to leave. Be highly sensitive to nonsense in your life, do not get used to it! If you numb yourself to it, again, you are adding insult to injury, neglect on top of abuse or neglect. This is self-harm, the kind of path you want to quickly get off of.

Not knowing how to challenge abuse or neglect does not excuse you from the responsibility to challenge it. Your life is entrusted to you, and you must learn how to protect it, so you may thrive. Only you can do this, no one else is in charge of the life of an adult person. If it means having to learn new skills, getting the necessary supports, and even making sacrifices in the name of health, do it. It is more than OK, it is your duty and responsibility to keep yourself safe, and even leave an abusive or traumatizing situation, job, or partner, if nothing else works. Not knowing how to do it is not an excuse in a society that provides counseling, support and even shelter for people who are victimized. You must take the initiative to reach out for help, even if this means making sacrifices - like losing a house or money. Safety is the most fundamental necessity, something only you can give to yourself. It is the first step in healthy self-parenting; once you have that, you can start building the rest on a solid foundation.

Reflection:

Is your tolerance for unnecessary pain too high? Tweak it down by becoming more sensitive, more in tune with your feelings.

Are you still with me? Hang in there, we *are* getting to the actual "protocol" for self-love, but first, we must address a few more things. Any time you feel we are on the same page about the foundations, our basic belief about self-love and self-care feel free to jump to the chapter Your Steps to Self-Parenting with Love.

Your Inner Vigilante

Delight in vigilance.
Protect your own mind.
Lift yourself from a bad course
Like a tusker sunk in mud.
The Dhammapada

Notice any manifestations of abuse or neglect in your relationship to yourself, in the way you act, talk, and think in front of your "Inner Child" – remember, awareness is the key to a good life. This will help you to obliterate your "blind spot", the pattern(s) that you are so used to, you don't even notice any more (you will find more on this in Part Four).

You can learn to become hyper-aware and sensitive to picking up on things that make you feel uncomfortable, and then quickly correct them, or shun them. *Consider any act, or even thought that is mean or neglectful in any way your most dangerous enemy: it will rob you of self-esteem, confidence, joy, strength, hope and in general, everything you ever needed.*

THAT, my friend is cause for alarm, and the best place to invest energy and time in.

You may think of it as a deadly germ, well, wouldn't you keep your house spic and span to avoid it? Your mental space is your house. Your body is your house. Keep them clean from these disease-disasters. Again, remember, you can only help what you know about: so be vigilant, and on the lookout for any of the following "suspects" in your inner territory (this is just a partial list): put them on your (un)Wanted List.

Signs of abuse or neglect in your relationships with others:

- fighting
- violence
- name-calling
- blaming
- shaming
- judging / criticizing
- lack of physical safety
- lack of emotional safety
- silence / distancing
- no affection
- no conversation / sharing of feelings
- no sex
- no time for each other
- negativity

Signs of abuse or neglect in your relationships to yourself:

- self-blame
- self-criticism
- self-judgment

- self-harming behaviors (cutting, addictions to food, alcohol, drugs, gambling, internet, gaming)
- anger
- reactivity (frustrated, irritable, annoyed)
- physical self-neglect
- emotional self-neglect
- over-working / driven-ness
- need to please
- no rest
- no hobbies/playtime
- no time with friends
- emotional problems (depression, anxiety, phobias)
- no time for Self
- negativity

Now that you have identified the bugs in your system, allow them to do just that: to bug you, to irritate you. Let yourself feel the discomfort they cause. This is very important, because if you numb your feelings, what in the world will remind you that there is a problem that needs your attention? So be vigilant, notice them and let them bother you, just enough to keep you alert and active in working to mop them out of your life. Your discomfort will not let you be complacent!

My Kind Companion, You have all the controls within your reach: focus inward, be informed and kind to yourself. This inner connection will spark the magic in your relationships as well.

Your Baseline of Discomfort

Many people ask me: "What's wrong with me?" My honest answer to most of them is "Nothing! You just have a high threshold of tolerance for unnecessary pain". Do *you*?

I often meet people who have made their lives into a four hundred pound gorilla that they have to feed every day, and think that there is no other way to live. There is. You are the boss of your life, and thus, you can pick your priorities. Pare your activities down and recognize that your joy, life force, and enthusiasm are your most valuable assets.

In order to eliminate unnecessary stress from your life it helps to take a fresh look at the amount of discomfort and pain you are willing to live with. We all have a "baseline of discomfort", the measure of pain we consider normal, not necessarily because it is, but because we are used to it.

Are you used to working too hard, running around, or feeling bad about yourself, physically hurting, or being exhausted? If so, do you notice it?

We humans operate on habit - and we should. Habit saves us energy, so we don't have to waste any of it figuring out how to brush our teeth or do all the automatic activities we perform each day. Trouble is, we can have some pretty destructive automatic mechanisms – a.k.a. bad habits - built into our systems. Even beyond those little suckers, take a look at the fundamental automatic setting you are operating on: where is your baseline of discomfort? In other words, *how much stress, pain (physical or emotional), chaos, or unhappiness are you willing to tolerate in your life?*

If that childhood of yours was not all peaches and cream chances are you have a high level of tolerance for pain, at least on some accounts. For instance, depending on how you were treated as a child you may not notice being and feeling ignored, invisible, or yelled at, criticized, or blamed. So today, you may consider these normal, and may not be challenging these behaviors and feelings – which, of course, perpetuates the cycle. Perhaps you did not get enough attention as a child, and are now putting up with negative attention, because it is more than no attention? These patterns will not change unless you make them an issue, and ask for what you *really* need to feel good.

> *Chad's childhood was filled with chaos, and parents screaming and putting him down. It is small wonder that today, at 35, when he could have a wonderful life, he is re-creating this familiar "baseline" of stress by having a troubled relationship and beating his body up with extreme sports. This realization helped him to re-set (i.e. lower) his baseline of tolerance for stress by actively and deliberately seeking out peaceful and positive experiences.*

Perhaps as a child, you *had to* develop a high tolerance for discomfort in order to make it through while staying as safe as possible. The good news is, now you don't have to put up with anything that hurts you! And you still may be putting up with it, because of the same old fears from your childhood (what if he or she gets mad / leaves me / won't love me / will judge me / will drink / gets sick?) Because of these old, outdated fears you are projecting your old situation onto your current one. Not good! Don't do it! Your partner (or spouse, or friend) is *not* your mom or your dad, or your uncle or cousin who hurt you. Your partner (or spouse, or friend) is the one you chose, and who supposedly loves you. Chances are he or she is willing and able to learn something new - you being the one and only potential teacher of what pleases you!

Very often the very fears that kept you safer in childhood may now be in your way of building a happier, more peaceful life. At this point, those fears are doing nothing more than masking your true needs, blocking you from noticing and feeling them, like a bodyguard left here from a previous regime. *Now is the time to learn what to do with those fears and how, so you may actually experience your feelings and go from there to create that better, healthier, more authentic life.*

More often than not we will inadvertently re-create the same level of stress in our lives that we had been used to. We will stir the pot, bring in chaos, bad company, or problems just to feel the way we are used to feel. We drag in and put up with the nonsense.

Do you know how to tolerate feeling good, and peaceful? Close and emotionally intimate? Have you ever felt this way long enough for your system to build it in as a blueprint, and tolerate it, rather than reject it as a foreign object? If you feel you do not have the blueprint for how to feel *great* you must give yourself permission *now* to feel good for long enough to relax with it, and absorb it into your body memory. Practice, my dear, and it will come easy as pie!

Taking it home:

In order to re-set your baseline of discomfort you will need to use a new point of reference.

- Find the number 0-10 (worst to best) of your general level of discomfort NOW, and then
- Choose the target number, the one you would like to have as your baseline;
- Sit comfortably, close your eyes, take a deep breath and relax your body;
- Think of a time in your life when you felt good, safe, relaxed; allow yourself to be transported to that time, and notice what feelings and sensations you have in your body, and where?
- Stay a few minutes in this state, re-absorbing the experience into your cellular memory, and

- Think of or see the target number. Tell yourself: "From now on _____ (your target number) is my baseline. When I feel less than this, I will notice it and do something about it!"
- Take out your journal or a piece of paper and write down in bullet points all the things you can do now - and on the long run - to reduce or eliminate stressors in your life. Post it in a conspicuous place – better yet, put these tasks into your schedule.

Make up your mind about this: take charge of your own happiness and health by becoming aware, and by making a conscious decision on how much abuse or neglect is OK in your life. (Hint: NONE!) Work on this a bit and you will be rewarded in spades!

Depression – Disconnect Central

You are not depressed, you are distracted.
Facundo Cabral

I don't know anybody who doesn't know somebody suffering from depression. The jury is still out on what exactly causes depression: nature or nurture? Is it genetic or is it a result of life experiences? This is truly a complex issue; I think it is both. Findings in epigenetics show that the brain is plastic: it can adapt and develop new neural connections - as a result of life experiences - that in turn may then infiltrate the DNA and be handed down to the next generations via genes. There is also new evidence that a healthy attachment early in life to a primary caretaker results in developing more neuropeptides. This means that the person will be more resilient in his lifetime to stress, anxiety, depression, and even trauma.

In my experience depression is the epitome of the downward spiral or the self-fulfilling prophecy of every negative thought, feeling and action, and thus, it is a true trap that requires professional help to unlock.

More often than not, depression comes about by a person being chronically disconnected from their feelings of pain. Cut off from the pain, the person loses his access to joy as well. In fact, pain and joy are like pearls on a string: cut the string, and you lose all your pearls (but not your marbles, I hope!). When the inner Self, the soul does not get what it needs, it will be starved and get depressed. When the parent is not home, the kids go awry.

When you shoot a zebra in the black stripe,
the white dies too;
shoot it in the white
and the black dies too.
South African Proverb

In our modern world depression has assumed epidemic proportions. This makes sense: distracted by the rat-race of too many work hours, commitments, and the exorbitant speed of information exchange courtesy of the media, our phones and electronics we live in profound disconnect from our feelings.

Depression affects about 15 million American adults or approximately 5 to 8% of the adult population in a given year. There are a few widespread myths circulating about the nature of this debilitating social ill we call depression. Lay people often think of it as severe sadness, a feeling of being downtrodden, tired, and upset. This is only partially true: depression is mostly not sadness, it is

EMPTINESS.

It is a profound disconnect from one's Self, from one's feelings - which is probably the most painful feeling anyone can experience. The main symptoms of depression are anxiety, worry, indecisiveness, inconsolable sadness, anger, feelings of worthlessness, hopelessness, and emptiness, guilt, shame, self-blame, pains and aches, self-isolation, and uncontrollable crying. In more serious cases sleep and appetite are also affected.

For the most part there are very good reasons for disconnecting from one's feelings - reasons that have precious little to do with genes. The main culprits are:

- Abuse, past or present (physical, emotional, or sexual) where the person feels there is no recourse;
- Neglect, past or present (emotional, or physical) where the person feels there is no recourse;
- Trauma (past or current):
  - physical (accidents, being a victim of, or witnessing violence)
  - emotional (bullying, or being called names, criticized, blamed, put down, ridiculed in a way that is or was both unbearable and inescapable to the sufferer);
  - sexual, or
  - any experience that was unbearably painful and inescapable at the time;
- Loss that has not been grieved adequately, a.k.a. unresolved grief (including even the loss of a relationship that was not happy, or of a job, house, childhood, youth, or of an occupation, role in life, etc.);
- Socialization: some cultures and religious groups expect their members to not feel, or not express their feelings;
- Family dysfunction: the person feels there is no recourse for his pain due to broken trust, addiction, chronic illness or mental illness in the family.

These are the most likely reasons why someone would unconsciously, but effectively shut down their feelings of pain. Among them loss is one of the most normal, therefore common reasons for disconnecting from one's feelings. Losing someone or something always hurts, it is a psychic wound that needs some attention to heal. Otherwise, it will go underground, and become a host for emotional "bacteria" to accumulate, and potentially pervade the whole system, at a future time, when something else happens that is painful.

I am all for antidepressants for severe, debilitating depression. For your garden variety chronic, low-grade depression the only wholesome, authentic – and might I add lasting - way out is listening to it, even though it hurts. When you listen, you are replete with your pain, which is the opposite of emptiness.

Pills numb the pain, thus taking the listening, understanding, and then helping part out of the equation. So do people who get depressed: this is not to blame, it is just a fact. You do not need medication in order to numb the pain; you can just shut it all down. People do this when they feel that the pain is too intense for them to handle, or they do not have the safety, supports, permission, or resources to feel and express it. Very often people judge themselves for feeling bad, and think that it is bad, and so they talk themselves out of it by calling themselves selfish, stupid, spoiled, or lazy.

Thus, medication may inadvertently collude with the depressed person's denial and refusal of their feelings - and perpetuate it to boot! When meds are prescribed for depression that is mild to moderate, the implicit messages can be profoundly disempowering:

- it is wrong to feel pain;
- there is no solution other than to numb the pain;
- there is nothing you can do about this;
- feeling pain is not OK;

-   you don't have what it takes, therefore you must reach for second best, which is not feeling.

Talk about defeating the purpose! Thus, medicating for milder depressions runs the risk of an ironic "side-effect": it will perpetuate it. This, by locking the sufferer into a vicious cycle:

Feeling bad → pills → not feeling → not doing what it takes to feel better (and not taking responsibility for it!) → pills to keep the depression at bay → not feeling, etc., you catch my drift.

For Major Depression, however, the type that interferes with your daily functioning of sleeping, eating and working meds *are* necessary to help to replenish on a daily basis, so you can learn to listen to your pain, and let it guide you into new ways of thinking and acting, ones dictated by your inner wisdom.

Be patient. Stay present, tuned in, attentive. Our accelerated culture could not be more unfriendly to these qualities, therefore it takes special practices to carve out the opportunity and build up the skills to tune inward.

To heal a chronic, low-grade depression (called Dysthymia) it is best to stay sensitive, lean into your feelings, and let them guide you out of the tunnel. It takes time, patience, humility. It will draw on, as well as build your ability to be honest, strong, ask for help, receive, and share - and it will work.

In the overwhelming majority of cases depression is the result of a *learned* disconnect from one's feelings. Feelings, intuition, or sensation are produced by the body's survival intelligence to prompt us to do what it takes to feel better. If the person does not notice, or accept the animal instinct in his body there will be a disruption in the information pathway. Illness is unavoidable if you are out of the loop, therefore unable to help yourself by doing the next healthy thing.

The remedy? Connecting with your feelings, without distractions. The best practices involved are solitude, time spent in nature, journaling, yoga and meditation. At times, cloistering, that is spending a longer period of time alone, preferably in Nature may be necessary. The A-B-C-D system described in this book is the synthesis of the best methods for inner connection.

Many people are unfamiliar with solitude, the quality of spending time in splendid isolation, even if just for an hour a day. Being alone is the soil from where the flower of self-love and appreciation blossoms. Many people are afraid, or at least uncomfortable with spending time alone – almost as if they were in a room with a stranger. You must spend time with that stranger, and get to know her. She is your best ally, remember? This is what it takes to learn to listen to your subtle – and not so subtle - longings, so you may honor them. As you let yourself have preferences on the small scale, your inner Self will not have to scream in pain to get your attention.

If you or someone you know is depressed definitely seek out professional help! This is to get a thorough assessment as to the possible causes of the depression. There are some causes that you simply cannot clear up on your own – no one could. Trauma (including a history of abuse and neglect), and unresolved grief are on the top of that list. Let a mental health professional help you with accessing those underlying feelings, that way you can get un-stuck from the frozenness of trauma and grief, and on your way to reconnecting with your Self. Any good psychotherapy will help with this reconnection. In my opinion the four-step Authenticity Method is the quickest way to do this. It will help you to stay connected and thrive in all ways.

Commit, Dearest to learn the skills it takes to be well. With practice, your life will be transformed beyond your wildest imagination.

PART THREE

Connection

I honor those who try
To rid themselves of any lying,
Who empty the self?
And have only clear being there.
Rumi

Connection Is Health

I can give this to you writing (in fact, I am!): the best remedy to the angst of being a human is a wholesome connection with ourselves. When our attention is focused inward we acknowledge the micro that carries the whole of the macrocosm, and thus we are aligning ourselves with Nature. We build a consciousness bridge, from the inside out, with the Universe that we are an organic part of. This is the essence of spirituality.

The most fundamental relationship we will ever experience is the one with our own Selves. It is an *actual* relationship. You are the one bathing, dressing, and feeding yourself. You are the one who talks to yourself, with a running commentary on everything you do, your circumstances, job, marriage, children, and your life. Are you treating yourself kindly? Are you being supportive, positive, loving to your Self? Or are you scornful, negative, absent or fear mongering?

> *My friend David Schechter, a Broadway writer gave me permission to share this with you: he told me the story behind an interesting looking ring he wears on his finger: he gave it to himself years ago, when he decided to "marry himself". No, really! He said he had been critical and hostile to his own self for so long he decided to put an end to the strife by this symbolic act of peace-making. He swears that since that day he has been feeling a lot more peaceful.*

David is onto something. The way we treat ourselves matters, it really does. It is a blueprint for how to be in the world; it has the power of a programming, a precedent that we will continue to repeat and extend to others, a model for how to be and behave. Indeed, we cannot overstep our shadows, we will give as much love, understanding, acceptance, kindness to those around us as we already give to ourselves. Same goes for criticism, sarcasm, blame, rejection, and all the other junk, like ignoring and abandonment.

If we look deep inside people's ways of relating we will find three fundamental types, three basic communication styles, whether with our Selves or with someone else:

1. Abuse (i.e. aggression, fight reaction, reactivity, disconnect)
2. Neglect (i.e. passivity, flight reaction, reactivity, disconnect)
3. Care (i.e. love, presence, responsiveness, connection)

The first two styles, abuse and neglect disconnect. The third one connects you with your feelings, your truths right here and now. You must develop the ability to feel, notice your feelings, and accept them as your guidance.

Don't be fooled by what everybody says; the problem in life is not that we feel bad. Life is stressful, and we will naturally feel bad in very many ways, for very many reasons. Stress is normal, and so is feeling bad. The problem is caused by what we do with our bad feelings. *The key to health, be it physical, emotional, or relational is what we do in response to how we feel. This is the moment of the truth.*

Do you approve or reject your feelings? Do you follow through with appropriate action to help yourself to feel better? More specifically:

1. Do you blame (criticize, judge) yourself for feeling stressed? If so, this is a setup for abusive relationships, and conflicts. You will be misunderstood, because your message to yourself and others is that they are "no good" - instead of what you really mean, which is that you need help.

2. Do you ignore (shut down, withdraw, isolate, abandon) yourself when feeling stressed? If so, this is breeding grounds for depression, anxiety, substance abuse, and mental or physical illness. It will cut you off from yourself - OUCH! – The most painful of mutilations. You will not get your needs met, because no one can read your mind, therefore they cannot be delivering to your needs, no matter how much they love you or how well they know you. You are not transparent, so no one can read your mind!

3. Do you accept the way you feel with compassion and patience? If you do, you are on the right track: you will help yourself, because now you are informed about what will actually help you to feel better. You will also be available for others, which is the way to nurture mutually happy relationships.

Do choose health over disease! Connect to your own true feelings, and then live by them. I will humbly guide you back to your formidable inner guidance. Follow me.

Feelings: Hug Them? Kick Them?

Your feelings are not more nor less than your truth in this moment. True is what *is*, while Right is what we think of as good and helpful. True is a thing of Nature, Right is man-made. You cannot judge True, because it is neither good, nor bad: it just is.

How you feel is a thing of Nature. We don't choose our feelings, they just are what they are: they come and go according to our momentary physical, mental and emotional states, much like the weather. Our feelings represent our internal climate. If we could choose how we feel, if we could mess with our instincts, we would be long extinct. In fact, *when it comes to feelings and needs, their truth is an indication of what is good and right at the moment.* The goal is to bring our thoughts – what we think of as right – in synch with our feelings, i.e. with what is.

Feelings serve survival, and survival is good – wouldn't you agree?

> *Seth told me that if feelings don't lie, then it is true that he is stupid and incompetent, because that is the way he feels. Whoa! Let's stop right there: what is true is that he feels that way, and not that he is stupid or incompetent. The feeling must be accepted, because he truly feels less than good enough. Only once he accepted his feelings can he go on to soothe himself, and then get the help he needs to heal those hurt feelings. If he did not accept his feelings <u>as his truth</u>, he would not do what it takes to feel better (e.g. to refuse the insult)! Instead, he would pile the insult of rejecting the feeling onto the injury of feeling it.*

You must take care that you yourself notice and validate your feelings, needs, or preferences, and not question or temper with their truths. Allowing yourself to feel bad is necessary for health - for too many reasons to count. Fundamentally, it validates the truth with compassion, which is love, and love is medicine. Love is THE medicine.

In the willingness to feel,
There is healing. In the
Choice not to closet, cast
Aside or deny experience,
Energy is freed, and I

Dive deeper into life.
Dana Faulds

Ellie is 28 going on 60; she feels spent, unenthusiastic, and always thinks of the worst case scenario. She told me with an edge in her voice and a 'tude in her posture that she did not want to pay attention to her feelings, no sir, and that's that. Feelings suck, she said, they just make you feel worse, and it's hard work, and scary to face them, and they take a lot of time and energy, and commitment, it's like going to the gym: "I know it's good for me, but I refuse." She said she knows she should, but she is afraid it will make her feel worse, before helping her to feel better. I said to her that the way to think of her feelings is that she is in the same house with a stranger, whom she needs to get to know, so they can get along, and cooperate. She said that's swell, since she likes to talk to people and get to know them!

Here is a partial list I gathered in my clinical work of the many reasons why we may suppress our feelings. Does any of these apply to you?

- it's what I learned as a child (from parents behavior or from having been punished for expressing your feelings)
- it is "unimportant" (minimizing one's Self)
- it is "selfish" (judging one's Self)
- I am afraid of others' reactions (being brushed off, ridiculed, invalidated, blamed)
- I don't want to burden anyone
- I think of my feelings as weakness
- I hope it will go away
- I am used to feeling bad
- I am afraid of conflict
- I am afraid of hurting others

- I want to disappear to avoid trouble
- I don't know how to express it
- My feelings are too intense: what if I go crazy?
- I don't want to turn into _____ (crazy relative's name)
- I don't want to be at the center of attention
- I never learned what to do with my feelings, so I don't pay attention to them
- I don't have a right to feel
- There is no time to feel
- I don't want to feel sorry for myself
- I don't want to be selfish
- I should think of others first
- I don't want to be lazy
- _____(fill in the blank)

If you believe any of the above, read on, and I will try to massage them out of your system.

Make friends with your feelings, Dear Reader: they will always guide you right.

Is Feeling Bad Negativity?

"I always thought of letting go as letting go of my feelings, and not as accepting them" – Jody said. She nailed a very common misconception: that we must "deal with" something difficult by sucking it up, and cutting off our feelings. True dealing (and strength) lies in the leaning into the feelings, and letting them guide you. If your boss gives you an assignment to "deal with", does that mean you must ignore it? You would lose your job in no time. Dealing with something literally means to engage with it and work with it, and go through the process toward a resolution, by taking into consideration the information the thing brings to the table. How do you deal with your finances? Your car troubles? Do you ignore the actual situation, the information inherent in it, or do you work with it? Don't answer, it's a poetic question.

Feeling bad is normal, what's more, it is necessary. Everybody feels bad (tired, overwhelmed, sad, worried, angry, etc.); the trick is to learn to address how you feel, instead of reacting to it. Negativity is talking yourself *out of* feeling is bad, which will lead you to react in anger or judgment or fear to the mere fact that you are feeling bad. This way you are in effect blocking the natural flow of your feelings, going against nature. Allowing yourself to feel uncomfortable is not negative, or dwelling, like we are often taught to think. As I hope you understand, it is actually helpful, because it nudges us toward the next healthy behavior that we would ONLY perform IF we felt badly.

Therefore, letting yourself feel whatever it is you are feeling at any given moment in time is necessary, and definitely not something you should frown upon – unless you are in the business of shouting at the rain to stop, or running into walls head-on.

Negativity is thinking badly of feeling bad. It will keep you stuck feeling bad, because it distracts from the message the discomfort is trying to convey to you (by judging, or ignoring it) and thus, from healthy action. As your attention and acceptance of the discomfort are derailed, the pain will escalate: there will be guilt on top of discomfort, adding another layer of hurt, insult to injury. It is like getting glued to the grime. *Do not try this at home!*

When you are stuck with the pain, you spiral down: there is more pain, more complaining and negativity, which can lead to substance abuse. "Poor me, poor me, pour me another one" – you've got to love the AA vernacular!

There is a difference between allowing yourself to feel bad for a little while (just long enough for this feeling to inform you about what your next healthy action should be), and dwelling, or allowing yourself to sink and drown in your sorrow, without doing anything to help yourself in a healthy way. Your inaction signals that you have panicked about feeling bad, and either "checked out", or launched into self-criticism about it. These are the two ways to be negative; using either you are throwing in the towel when you feel bad.

When you quell your sadness the messenger is dead, and the country is in the throes of trouble. Feelings are blocked in order to prevent pain, and what ensues is more intense pain: a sort of insult to injury.

Being positive, on the other hand, means letting yourself feel bad, and then taking care. Thus, pay attention, believe your feelings, let them inform you about what to do to feel better, and then, do just that.

Needs: The Free Radicals

God picks up the reed-flute world and blows.
Each note is a need coming through one of us,
A passion, a longing-pain.
Remember the lips
Where the wind-breath originated,
And let your note be clear.
Don't try to end it.
Be your note.
I'll show you how it's enough.
Rumi

I like to think of needs as hungry free radicals frantically searching for their exact match. A feeling of sadness requires solace, and not food, or anything else - if you know what I mean. Funny thing is, we are radically free in deciding whether or not we will give ourselves that exact match. Truth be told, this is the only freedom, the only control we have in life. Think about it, realize it, and then, come back home to do what you can to feel better. Forget about trying to control anything else: it cannot be done.

> *Jill overeats and would so much like to lose some weight, but she cannot. No matter what she tries to do, the weight stays, only to increase over time. She eats every time she feels uncomfortable, even when she is not hungry. She gives herself food instead of all the things that she really needs: when she is tired, she does not rest: she eats, when worried, she does not talk to someone: she eats, and so on. If being stuck in this self-numbing pattern were not painful enough, she also hates herself, and verbally abuses herself for it.*

Obviously, this very sad, addicted way to live deserves compassion, not judgment - even, and *primarily* from herself! If this was a child crying, would you just shove food in her mouth, or would you try to find out what is amiss and then give her that? Over-eating, as well as any other addictive behavior is a substitute for the thing we REALLY need, and as such, it will NEVER hit the spot. It will temporarily numb the discomfort and distract from it, only for the pain to come back later – and this time, with a vengeance. It is like a generic drug, for a very specific ailment, or like taking a common antibiotic for a specific strain of bacteria: the symptoms will temporarily dissipate, only to erupt later, only worse.

Our needs act the same way. Remember, they are the *truth*, and as such they are not going anywhere, until they get acknowledged and met. Substitutes will numb, but never satisfy; hence the obsessive repetition of the act, in the hopes that *this* time it would work. Repeating the behavior over and over will form a habit, and now we are having to fight the habit on top of learning to tolerate feeling uncomfortable, slowing down to inquire within, and then give ourselves directly what we need.

That is five steps removed from healthy, quite a lot to handle. Still, so long as you understand what you must do to be healthy, you can step on that path and practice those behaviors - long enough, mind you, to form a habit of it. This will replace the old compulsion(s), and pave the way for healthy living.

Only a patient, open and honest inquiry into your feelings will lead to the information about what you really need to be well on our journey. We get addicted to the substitutes because they do bring temporary relief, and because a lot of people do not have faith that they have a right to receive what they need, and that this is possible, with no compromise. Faith, and then persistence, because you will only get what you actually reach for and insist upon.

Substitutes are on the bottom shelf in the food store, where the junk food is, they are easier to reach than the things on the top shelves where the good stuff is. It takes time, patience, focus, humility, faith, perseverance, as well as support, and even guidance to be able to reach there - and keep reaching there. Living in this authentic way draws upon your character, and then strengthens it in spades.

> *A Joke: Mr. Smith prays to God, day in and day out, please, God, let me win the lottery, please!!! After a few weeks of this, God appears to him, saying, "Okay, Mr. Smith, I will, but do me a favor: buy a ticket!"*

My Gentle Reader, if you recognize yourself in this, and know that you have been reaching for substitutes, take heart: you can have everything that you need. All you have to do is reach for it!

Do You Want What You Need? - Needs VS Wants

You might think this is a joke, but I swear, it really did happen. I asked Mrs. Jones how come she was still smoking, despite of having been diagnosed with lung cancer?
She replied: You don't want me to harm myself, do you? Every time I quit smoking, my blood pressure goes up!

Many people confuse their needs with their wants (as in "I need that Gucci bag!") In our society we mostly live by our wants. Very often wants are dictated by the mind, scrambling to find a solution to our different hungers, alias needs - something it cannot access. So it comes up with blind guesses, second best solutions. Needs, on the other hand live in the body. Given the franticness of our mind-activity that this culture promotes, you may have trouble tapping into them in your typical, everyday frame of mind.

There is nothing wrong with what you want, with ambition and desires, as long as it is not a *replacement* for unfulfilled needs. Sometimes people want money, position, power or fame in order to get what they need: peace of mind, safety, respect, attention, or just to feel loved. As we all know, those wants do not necessarily meet these needs.

Of course, it is a good thing to strive for wealth, and power, if that is what you truly need, because you have a talent that is bursting and must be manifested. Oftentimes, however, these are just substitutes, stand-ins for the real things. *Anything you need you can get directly, granted you know how. It requires that you be authentic by aligning your thoughts and actions with the way you really feel.* And then, but only then, you can have the closest thing to a guarantee that your needs *will* be fulfilled.

Happiness comes with your ability
to manifest first your smallest desires,
and later your biggest dreams.
Paramhansa Yogananda

No wonder there is so much confusion in people's heads about what they want as opposed to what their true needs are. Our consumerist society is certainly doing its best to foster this confusion. Marketing professionals are explicitly taught to manipulate people into thinking that they actually need what they perhaps never even knew they wanted – a glittery pair of shoes, a certain type of candy bar, etc. This practice is by now an intrinsic part of our everyday culture, perpetuated by the media, as well as peer pressure. The net result is that too many people accept external guidance for what they need, thus losing touch with the only one we actually have: our intuition that lives in our bodies.

If you are not addicted to anything, here is a sure-fire way to discern whether a craving is a want or a need:

1. let yourself feel the feeling;
2. rate its intensity from 1 (weak) to 10 (strong);
3. if it is a 7 or more, it is probably a need;
4. accept it as your truth!
5. assert it to the people around you, and make sure you are heard (see more on assertiveness in the corresponding chapter).

Do you notice how you feel when you get exactly what you need? Peace, joy, health and love follow closely in the footsteps of true self-care. You feel connected to yourself, and all is well. We all know how it feels to act on wants *instead* of our needs: after the initial distraction, there is frustration, discontent, maybe even guilt or shame. Good thing is, needs have the annoying habit of not leaving until they are fulfilled; they go dormant, and then erupt with the wrath of an angry God when you least expect it. Hey, we can run, but we cannot hide. The truth of our feelings and needs is like a diamond, nothing cuts through it.

I encourage you, Dear Reader, to want to feel, trust your needs, and meet them. Will you?

Addictions

Oftentimes people use second best solutions when they feel bad. Here are some examples for how wants can short-circuit getting what you need:

FEELING	NEED = Addressing	WANT = Avoiding or Distracting
	Examples	Examples
Tired	Rest with no stimulation	Watch TV, stimulation
Lonely	Honest conversation	Go to bar, look at porn
Hungry	Nutritious food	Junk food
Angry	Conflict resolution	Break something
Sad	Consolation	Withdraw, isolate
Worried	Reassurance, positive self-talk	Complaining, negative self-talk
Anxious	Soothing company, or activity, self-soothing	Pills, alcohol/drugs
Exhausted	Vacation	"Stay-cation", Doing chores

Depressed	Feel, inquire within, address counseling, lifestyle changes (sleep, exercise, nutrition, rest, relationships), meds?	Pills, alcohol/drugs
Grief	Grieving, counseling sharing	Overworking, distractions, blame someone or one's Self
Stressed	Relax, share	Eat something
Frustrated	Breathe, assert yourself	Fight, or flight
Empty	Ask for affection/love	Eat, drink

Those suffering from addictions often use these to feel free, to not be confined by their lives that became just obligation, or reprimand, and not a lot of fun. What they really need is freedom, time off and fun, and un-structured activities, but they do not give themselves permission for that, so they eat, drink, or use drugs as a way to legitimate taking time out for themselves ("If I eat, I am excused, one must eat!" or: "If I am drunk, I cannot work, sorry!")

Addictions have a lot to do with lack of assertiveness: the less the person asks for what they need, the less they receive it, the less they receive it the more they hurt, the more they hurt, the bigger the need for numbing the pain. This opens the door for all sorts of addictions, which are a way to avoid asking for help, and giving one's self something, instead of nothing. Unfortunately, that something will add another problem on top of the original one.

These substitute-activities are also a symbolic representation of things being out of balance: over-eating is an indication of being "starved" for something the person is not getting. Abusing alcohol is an indication of needing "time out", to be "out of commission", away from the pressures (mostly self-imposed) and not always be perfect and engaged. Gambling indicates a need to play and take some risks, and not live in constant fear of life. Drug abuse symbolically shows the person's need for boundaries, focus and structure, and it prompts everyone around them to feel such outrage, they rush in with attention and limit-setting (jail-time would be an extreme example).

Reactivity: Abuse or Neglect

The moment you feel bad is the moment of the truth: what you do at the moment of feeling uncomfortable will define your destiny. This is not an exaggeration. If you ask me how much control we have in life, I would say close to zero. Paradoxically, the only thing we can truly control is whether or not we accept our feelings. Exercising this freedom means choosing to *allow* - and step out of the way. When we do, things go well. When we don't, we go down.

Thus, when you feel discomfort you have two options: either go with it, connect with it, or go against it, and disconnect from your truth. Love is to go with, to accept that you are feeling bad, and listen to what you need from yourself to feel better. Love is responsive to the discomfort, like a parent to a child who just got hurt. By contrast, when you go against the way you feel (by ignoring or judging it) you are being reactive to your own discomfort – and either get mad *or* take off from the scene of the injury. Stop! Turn around! *You* are the doctor!

Reactivity is the opposite of "stepping back", or separating yourself from the stress. It is the fight or flight reaction we see in nature. Animals run (even by freezing), or attack when it's a matter of life or death. Running, in human terms is avoiding, distancing, ignoring. Attacking is blaming, judging, and criticizing. If you do either while stressed, if you attack or ignore yourself or others when stressed out, you are operating from your reptile brain, not your human brain, the neo-cortex. Truth is, feeling bad is not a life or death situation – therefore, reacting to feeling stress is like peeling an orange with a rifle. It will be peeled alright, with no orange left to tell the tale!

When we are reactive we get hurt on every level: because it adds stress on top of stress, our body, and relationships suffer first; top that with the damage it causes to our very hope in life.

Responsiveness is what works: it is slow, patient, mindful, and present. We human beings thrive when we are responsive to everyday stresses, because this stance allows us to get all of our needs met. The four steps to self-love (i.e. the ABCD protocol you will find in the chapter Your Steps to Self-Parenting with Love) is a detailed roadmap about how to be responsive, and find your way back to your true Self.

If you feel ready, do jump there now – or hang with me for a little while longer, and I promise, we shall get there soon!

Reactivity Quiz

Do you feel you have been reactive when you feel bad, physically or emotionally? Think of an uncomfortable situation, maybe from yesterday, and watch how you react to it. Chances are this is how you usually operate under stress:

A. *Fight Reaction:*

Under stress do you:

1. *Blame yourself or others (e.g. "Had I not shaken his hand, he would not have a cold!)*
    Always   Often   Rarely   Never

2. *Guilt yourself or others out of paying attention (e.g. "I don't want to be selfish" or "You are not the center of the world!")*
    Always   Often   Rarely   Never

3. *Scare yourself or others with negative thoughts and images (e.g. "What if I get cancer? What if you don't find a new job?)*
    Always   Often   Rarely   Never

4. *Do something to numb the feelings (drink, use drugs, gamble, overeat, shop, party, etc.)*
    Always   Often   Rarely   Never

5. *Physically hurt yourself or others (e.g. cutting, risky behaviors, violence)*
    Always   Often   Rarely   Never

6. *Should-ing yourself or others (e.g. "I should not feel this", or" You should stop reading and do something useful", etc.)*
    Always   Often   Rarely   Never

7. *Name-calling or negative labeling of Self or others (let me not cite examples)*
   Always   Often   Rarely   Never

8. *Acting out behaviors (sexually, or stealing, lying, cheating, tantrums, etc.)*
   Always   Often   Rarely   Never

B. <u>Flight Reaction</u>

Under stress do you:

1. *Do something to distract yourself or others (overwork, seek out company, shop, sleep, etc.)*
   Always   Often   Rarely   Never

2. *Postpone paying attention to your own or someone else's stress because there are more important things to do*
   Always   Often   Rarely   Never

3. *Minimize your own or someone else's feelings' importance*
   Always   Often   Rarely   Never

4. *Panic and run to a doctor with any small injury or pain*
   Always   Often   Rarely   Never

5. *Get anxious, worried or fearful of something terrible happening*
   Always   Often   Rarely   Never

6. *Catastrophize or generalize the situation (e.g. "this is terrible, you will never be able to..., I will always...")*
   Always   Often   Rarely   Never

7. *Isolate yourself or distance from others and get depressed*
   Always   Often   Rarely   Never

8. *Ignore the discomfort altogether*
   Always   Often   Rarely   Never

9. *Identify with the discomfort ("I AM this pain (or illness, or condition), there is nothing I can do about it")*
   Always   Often   Rarely   Never

10. *Focus your attention on someone else's need and ignore your own*
    Always   Often   Rarely   Never

If you answered "rarely" or "never" more than seven times you are in the clear with your self-parenting: it is wholesome, that is *responsive*! Keep it up, and you will be and stay healthy. You have been practicing what it takes to love yourself – and others - by being positive, present, and open under duress, and giving yourself and others what is needed for healing.

If you answered "often" or "always" mostly in group A you have been *reactive* to your feelings by becoming *aggressive* to yourself or others. When you over-react the discomfort, you get derailed from taking care of yourself, and, by extension, of others. This way of coping with pain is equivalent to the *fight reaction*. In relational terms this is what we call *abuse*. Somebody - in this case you - will get hurt, which results in even more injury. You felt bad in the first place, now you feel even worse, for instance, guilty for feeling angry, or hurt on top of sad, etc. Not fair! You deserve being *helped*, first and foremost by yourself when you don't feel well. Isn't that what you would do when someone you love is hurt? Your child, or parent, partner, or best friend? Bottom line is, when feeling hurt or stressed in ANY way, do not harm yourself or others, because then you will be tied into a Gordian knot. It is tantamount to giving up control.

If you answered "often" or "always" mostly in group B you have been *reactive* to your stress and discomfort by fleeing, becoming *passive*, throwing in the rains right when you should grab them to be well. If you abandon yourself in your discomfort, or let it take you over, that is insult to injury because you are not there to help yourself, or the other person, while the problem remains, and you are passively standing by witnessing someone, if just you, be hurt. This adds to the problem, because it damages your trust and confidence in your own Self. Self-abandonment leads to a lonely life. In relationships we call this stance *neglect*.

Here is a summary of the three ways we can be at the moment of feeling discomfort.

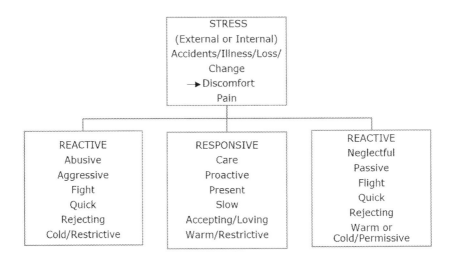

Responsiveness: An Authentic Connection

Being responsive means befriending your feelings, so they may guide you. Feelings express your authentic Self. Here is the definition of "authenticity" as per Wikipedia:

"Legitimate, genuine, valid. The word comes from Greek 'authentikos', meaning original, genuine, and principal. This comes from 'authentes', that is one acting on one's own authority, from 'autos', that is self, and 'hentes', meaning doer, being,". The sense of authentic as "entitled to acceptance as factual" is first recorded mid-14th C. Traditionally (at least since the 18th C.), authentic implies that the contents of the thing in question correspond to the facts and are not fictitious."

Being authentic is living, thinking, speaking and acting on the truth of how you feel inside. When you are real and genuine, you are being driven from your inner core, your own feelings and desires, and not from some outside source, like others' expectations or even your own bullying or fearful thoughts.

Being authentic is at the core of happiness. Happiness lays in the skill to take a step back from your own feelings, in order to be able to give yourself love, acceptance and compassion in the midst of pain, be it physical or emotional. This practice requires that the mind be present with the truth of the body, the soul, or the heart. As you accept and honor that truth, and treat yourself with kindness in the process you will experience equanimity, that is, an even keeled contentment and happiness. The operative word here is "step back": do not attach yourself to what you are feeling at the moment. If you identify with your pain, you will *be* the pain, reactive, with no one home to soothe you!

When you are responsive you practice the four steps of self-love, either automatically, or deliberately.

1. Attention to and acceptance of your feelings and body sensations;
2. Breathing and self-soothing with those sensations, long enough for you to be able to

3. Communicate with those sensations about how you feel and what you need, so that you may

4. Do it.

In a later chapter we will delve into the actual skills involved in being responsive – that is loving - to your Self, and to others. (Check out the Self-Parenting Questionnaire to see where you are at right now in your relationship to your Self.)

> *Just let yourself feel bad, will you? Feeling bad is normal; don't ignore or insult it. Keep your wound clean, and meet it with compassion and care: that is the way to be, and to get well.*

Spiral Up, or Spiral Down

Underneath all of our assumptions, doctrines and expectations there is a clean pool of wisdom: our intuition. It is pure and uncontaminated by our upbringing, an artesian well of deep knowing. This truth must be revered, noticed, accepted and followed. It is *always* at your fingertips. Here is a fact of life: when you encounter your discomfort with acceptance and love, you are being responsive, and things get better. When you meet it with scorn or a cold shoulder you are reactive, and they get worse.

feeling good, spiraling up into well-being
doing something positive about it
even more comfortable
positive self-talk/self-soothing
more comfortable
compassion and help

ACCEPTING SELF

FEELING UNCOMFORTABLE
(H.A.L.T. i.e. hungry, angry, lonely, tired)

REJECTING SELF
judgment or neglect
more uncomfortable
negative self-talk
even more uncomfortable
not doing anything or doing
something negative about it
spiraling down into depression

Until the next moment, when your feelings will change, morph, fluctuate and otherwise flow like they do because you are ALIVE. Like, or admit it or not, you are a high maintenance person - we all are. Self-care is a process, it must not stop, especially when you are not feeling good! Would you turn away from someone you love right at the moment they need your help the most? What would happen if you paid attention to how you feel pretty much throughout the day, and tethered yourself, by constantly giving yourself a soothing breath, a kind word, a positive gesture? Try it out, see how you feel then. Take full responsibility for helping yourself with how you feel, and don't wait for the world to rescue or deliver.

My Gentle Reader, you are fully equipped to meet yourself exactly where you are and to give yourself what you need to feel better - even if by asking for it. Take the next hour to try this on for size - and may that experience become a blueprint for the rest of your life!

This table shows how the three main dispositions manifest in the different aspects of your life.

Reactivity vs Responsiveness

AREA OF FUNCTIONING	REACTIVITY - FIGHT	REACTIVITY - FLIGHT	RESPONSIVENESS
Communication style	aggressive (blameful, critical, threatening, loud, violent, name-calling, swearing)	passive (quiet, withdrawn, pouting, sullen, uninvolved, indecisive, silent, absent)	Assertive (calm, friendly, clear, positive, specific)
Relationship style (with Self and Others)	abusive, unsafe, disconnected	neglectful, unsafe, disconnected	caring, connected, safe, intimate
Behavior under stress	confrontational	avoidant	proactive
General stance	closed	closed	open
Emotional stance	angry, fearful	fearful, frustrated	loving, peaceful
Outlook on life	negative	negative	positive
Physical state	tense	tense	relaxed
Mental State	unaware (of Self and Others)	unaware (of Self and Others)	aware (of Self and Others)
Thinking / Mental Activity	overactive, negative, misaligned with feelings and needs = invalidating (frustrated, angry, judgmental, excluding others, either/or = digital)	overactive, negative, misaligned with feelings and needs = invalidating (worried, anxious, judgmental, excluding Self, either/or = digital)	moderately active, positive, aligned with feelings and needs = validating (accepting, loving, caring, giving, including Self and Others, and/and = analog)

AREA OF FUNCTIONING	REACTIVITY - FIGHT	REACTIVITY - FLIGHT	RESPONSIVENESS
Physical Health	illness, pains, aches	illness, pains, aches	Healthy, pleasant physical sensations
Mental Health	explosive: anger issues, possible criminal behavior, mental illness	implosive: depression, anxiety, possible addiction, mental illness	well adjusted, balanced, healthy
Behavior	open, threatening, fighting, volatile	closed, distancing, withdrawn, isolating	open, peaceful, safe
Parenting Style	cold or hot restrictive	cold or warm, permissive	warm, restrictive
Relationship Style	conflicted, feuds, no boundaries (too close), intrusive	disengaged, schisms, cutoffs, distant (too far), excluding	connected, loving including
Coping under stress	doing, active, controlling, reactive	being, passive, absent, reactive	being with, proactive, present, responsive
Main coping tool	mind/thinking	mind/thinking	body/sensing, feeling, intuiting
Scope	survival	survival	thriving
Basic relationship to Self and Other	inauthentic, co-dependent or dependent	inauthentic, co-dependent or dependent	authentic, inter-dependent
Primary focus	external	external	internal
Attachment style	insecure, anxious, disorganized	insecure, ambivalent/resistant, avoidant	secure, reliable

Your Inner Child

There is a fundamental relationship, the one to our own Selves. It is the inner Self that guides us into wellbeing with its constant flow of information through sensations, urges, and images. You can call this inner Self many ways: your higher Self, your body's intelligence, your wise Self, your ancient Self. The way we relate to this part of us that represents our uncompromising drive to live and be well serves as a blueprint for all aspects of our lives. I like to think of it as the relationship between the Inner Parent that carries our thoughts, and the Inner Child, the carrier of our feelings. The Parent is the one in charge of taking care of us, the one that feeds, bathes, and clothes us, and hopefully says "no" when we are tempted to do something hurtful to ourselves. All this, with a running commentary on everything we do, feel, or think. Our Inner Child listens and acts accordingly, either by cooperating, or by rebelling. It all depends on the Inner Parent's style. Is your IC nice or naughty? Well, what is your IP like?

Neither the Child, nor the Parent is better – or more important - than the other: the former carries your true feelings, the latter knows right from wrong. They both contribute equally to your well-being. To be healthy and balanced you must forge a strong, open, mutually respectful, and loving relationship between them.

Your IC communicates with you incessantly through your body's sensations, about how you really feel - which, of course, is code for what you need to do to feel better. This, despite of what you *think* you should feel or not feel! He or she communicates through your body's sensations, as well as words, images and urges - and never lies. He or she carries the truth of who you are this very moment. You must learn to treat this Inner Child of yours with respect, love, and care. You must have a strong alliance with this part of you that holds the secrets to your well-being. You must learn to parent him or her in a way that promotes trust.

Are you mean- that is abusive - to yourself in *any* way? Do you criticize, judge, label, or even scorn, or distrust yourself? Do you harm your body with too much food, alcohol or drugs? Do you inflict injury on your body in any way, if not through frequent "accidents" and mishaps? If so, your Inner Parent is abusive. Conversely, do you lovingly soothe yourself, when in distress? If not, Your Inner Parent may be neglectful to your Inner Child. In return, the Inner Child part of you will act out: overeat, or starve, use drugs or alcohol, throw tantrums, overwork, overspend, gamble, etc. That ingenious Inner Child will do everything in its power to sabotage your dreams for a good life. It is truly brilliant, because this will likely cause so much upheaval and pain, that you will finally pay attention to what's going on, and hopefully make some fundamental changes. These changes, however, must not just be made on the level of behavior, but much deeper, on the level of the way you treat your feelings, the moment-by-moment instantaneous messengers of your Truth.

For instance, you have a headache. A thought would say, yeah, that's because I stayed up late last night. At that moment you have effectively shut your Inner Child up, as if you knew better what he was going to say. That's just a subtle way how you cut yourself off from your truth-source. If this was an actual child who is crying, would you say, I know, it's because your sister was mean to you? Well, what did you do to deserve it? If you jump to an interpretation or a judgment you are disconnecting from the truth, and will be lost as to what to do next, or you will do or say something that is not helpful, or even damaging.

So, we must learn to stay quiet, and listen. Let your IC talk to you, and tell you the truth about your feelings and needs. Without this asking and listening you would not know. There is a way to listen to your body's messages that will allow for the information to emerge clean, crisp and intact. This information is the only true guidance for what to do or say that is most helpful to you AND for everyone around you (even if they – or you - don't understand or like it).

My Beloved, the moral of the story is: notice and accept your Inner Child, who speaks to you through feelings, physical or emotional. He or she will inform and urge you toward the next healthy action. One authentic action at a time, and you can't help but be well!

PART FOUR

Connecting Through Self-Parenting

Knowing others is intelligence;
Knowing yourself is true wisdom.
Mastering others is strength;
Mastering yourself is true power.

Lao Tzu

Safety in Intimacy

Positive self-parenting of course will be warm and restrictive, just like the only effective style of parenting in child-rearing.

Warmth is that kind, positive attention and acceptance you give to someone you love, in this case to your Inner Child, carrier of your emotional truths. Embrace your feelings with compassion and unconditional love, just like you would (hopefully) respond to a child's feelings, whom you love.

Restrictive means establishing rules for yourself, like you would for a child you love. Rules are necessary for anything to be secure and safe – whether it is a country, a community, a marriage or ourselves – from negative thoughts, behaviors, and attitudes, lest our lives will be infested by them. When it comes to issues of safety and health these rules must not be negotiable.

My willingness to be intimate with my own deep feelings
creates the space for intimacy with another.
Shakti Gawain

When you parent yourself in a positive, loving way, you experience safety in a close, intimate relationship – with your own Self! One must have this experience from somewhere; if it was not from back home, it must be created and consistently experienced *now*. This will create and serve as a new model for life that will enable you to seek and maintain intimate relationships that are safe, while recognizing and accepting them.

An automatic pilot of positive self-parenting lays at the very foundation of healthy relationships.

Trust is the bedrock of a healthy relationship with one's Self. If you don't quite trust yourself yet, learn now to trust your feelings, or instincts, or body-sensations unconditionally. Trust the only reliable guidance you have in life; this requires paying attention, accepting, self-soothing with the truth of how you feel and going from there, thus, organically building your whole existence around this moment-by-moment truth.

Good news is, you can relax. Kick back, and stop fighting it. Nothing cuts through the truth, it is like a diamond! *The key to learning to trust the truth is to surrender to this ever-changing flow of information about how you feel, so you may give yourself what you need.*

If you are a religious person think of trusting you internal guidance as faith in God. You are being guided through your own body's signals. Whether or not you believe in God, do have faith that Life is guiding you into health and joy, at every step of the way, through the sensations and urges in your body.

> *From the time my daughter Julie was in second grade, we let her pick two days out of the school year when she could stay home, just because she felt she needed time for herself. She did not have to be sick to take avail of this privilege, just needing a break, as long as it was not the day of a test or exam. Our hope was to give her permission to trust her feelings and the experience of being listened to, accepted, without having to explain, so she may learn, or rather not forget to be connected within. You will be delighted to learn that she never once abused this privilege!*

The importance of cooperating with our own selves cannot be overstated. Inner conflict is the hotbed of emotional and physical illness. Even from the fundamental perspective of biology we can only survive, let alone thrive if we cooperate; we are collective beings, after all! This requires the ability to trust, that is to stay present, physically and emotionally when someone approaches us. Why? Because they have information we need to have in order to be able to cooperate.

Intimate encounters, however, come at the risk of getting hurt. The closer someone comes to us the more intimate the situation, and the higher the stakes when it comes to safety. In order to be able to cooperate we must allow people to come close. Being able to feel safe with and tolerate intimacy is a basic requirement for survival; we know this, because every human craves safe and close relationships. Even those of us most scared of intimacy would love to be able to tolerate it, because it is such an intrinsic human need.

In order to achieve safety in your relationship with your Self you must pay attention to your feelings in a positive way, and accept them as your truths. This is authenticity, the foundation of healthy self-parenting with love, because it allows you to align your thoughts and actions with this inner truth. This stance – and practice - is what leads to a healthy and happy life.

As you learn to parent yourself positively you are laying the foundation for a better, happier, and more sustainable life. Over time, and imperceptibly, you will develop the antennae necessary to notice the people, situations and circumstances that carry those positive qualities for you. You will lower your tolerance for negativity, and heighten your tolerance for intimate closeness, along with your intention to get what you need.

Establishing safety, positive attention, care and respect in your relationship with yourself will heal old wounds. And then, there is a bonus: self-love will also set you up for physical, emotional and relational health. I know people who were torn down as children, yet were always dreaming of a loving relationship – and then they found it! Love and acceptance in adulthood can also lead to healing.

We realize what we dream of, so do dare to dream, and then learn the skills to make your cravings come true. We all crave closeness, and that can only happen if it is safe. If I can make that happen with myself, then, I will know how it is done, and I will know what it feels like – and how to tolerate it. *Now*, I can hope and reach for it in my significant relationships. How to do this? Hang in there, we *are* getting to the ABCD's of self-love.

Alignment

Getting your needs met is a process – I call it positive self-parenting. It is easy to be tripped up on this road; certain misalignments among your feelings, thoughts, and actions will effectively block the way. The ABCD protocol will ensure that you stay on target with positive self-parenting, and undo any misalignment on the way.

Here is an image: picture yourself as a tree. Your roots are your instinct, or intuition, which manifests in the form of physical sensations. Sensation is compacted information for feelings and needs. So the sensations through your roots become the feelings in your trunk, which extend into your branches, which is your thoughts. They are meant to be in agreement with your feelings and needs (represented by your trunk), because by design they are merely a tool to resolve any problems in the way of getting the needs met. This is where we get stuck most often: when we let our thoughts disagree with our feelings (picture it as a breakage between the trunk and the branch). This creates an internal schism, a hopeless state of confusion, loss of direction, and as a result we are left deprived of what we really need to be well. In terms of the tree image the leaves and the flowers and fruits represent your beliefs, words, and actions. If these are in alignment with your feelings and needs, they are going to help you thrive; if not, they may hurt you.

Only feelings that are noticed and acknowledged will inform of needs. Only the needs that are noticed and accepted can be met. When the thoughts contradict, or invalidate the feelings, the tree will starve, there is a blockage, a thrombosis that can be lethal, if not to the physical body, certainly to your happiness...

Empty your mind of all thoughts.
Let your heart be at peace.
Lao Tzu

Abuse and neglect will drive your Inner Child into hiding or rebellion. Not cooperation, mind you. The goal is to find inner peace, and stop the battle between you and you, between your mind and your body. The mind is often negativistic, critical, or absent. The mind is the Inner Parent that must learn to treat your body with acceptance, love and respect. In fact, the body is the Inner Child, desperately and relentlessly trying to keep you alive and well. The Inner Child carries all the necessary information to be well, because it is intrinsically connected with Nature (or God, or the Universe, pick your choice of words).

You can, and must create a loving and cooperative relationship with your Inner Child. Listening to it equals listening to your body's signals. This is when you feel well and balanced – another way to say the "h" word: happy.

The goal is to re-align ourselves with the truth of how we feel. Since we don't choose our feelings, we are smart to oblige, and follow nature's rule, preferably without wasting much time and energy on questioning, doubting, judging or ignoring the truth. This is something the mind is very apt at: we have learned to give our thoughts the authority to run the show, like spoiled children in a chaotic household. We are indoctrinated to listen to our thoughts more than to our feelings, because they scream louder – as in "squeaky wheel gets the grease", right? Feelings are subtle at first, like a whisper. Later they can get "louder", more noticeable, because nature must and will escalate our pain, to make sure we pay attention. And even then, we are masters at ignoring, masking, denying, or otherwise dethroning them.

Healthy self-parenting starts with re-establishing authority to your feelings. This is done by paying attention to and accepting the subtle sensations in your body. To do this it may be necessary for you to change your reference point, from thinking to sensation. The body never lies. Learning humility and surrender to the truth of how you feel is not optional if you are to thrive: it is imperative! This will help you to synchronize your thoughts with your feelings, so you may know what to do next.

Exercising acceptance:
Describe an Object without Judgment

- *Choose a plain, everyday object, one right next to you now - a mug, a pen, a book, etc.*
- *Take a good, long look at it, and describe it in twelve short statements that are neither positive, nor negative, that is completely non-judgmental (e.g. this cup is decorated with flowers, has a handle, and it is painted blue on the inside).*
- *Watch for any judgmental statements, positive, or negative! (E.g. "It's ugly, but I like it...")*. *Practice accepting this object just the way it is.*
- *Now, spend a few minutes offering the same acceptance to yourself, just the way you are.*

You CAN create a safe connection with yourself Dear, by playing close attention to your feelings. You CAN change the way your life is, by healing your relationship to yourself FIRST. This is the foundation of your whole life - make it strong!

Internal Focus: Looking at your Blind Spot

Who looks outside, dreams; who looks inside, awakes.

Carl Gustav Jung

Rosemary was between a rock and a hard place when she came to see me. She was disenchanted with her husband of 10 years – mostly because she never asked for what she needed in a way he could hear. At this time she was engaged in an affair with another man. When it came to sign the divorce papers she balked: scared and confused, she did not know which direction to go. Her life brought her to a crossroads, where she was forced to take a stand and ask for what she needed – something she never did before. In order to move on with her life she had to really look inside, to her true feelings to find her own answer, rather than focus on others' needs – the very thing that got her into trouble in the first place.

You can only ask for what you need if and when you are aware of it, when you pay attention to how you feel. Your feelings know what you need, and signal them with their quality and intensity. If it is in your practice to ignore or judge your feelings (like your parents were when you were a child), you are likely to not notice the pain when others do it to you. Or, if you do, you may be too tentative in addressing it with the other person, because you may be used to feeling ignored or judged, so that makes it less of an issue for you. This is what we call a "blind spot". We cannot see things that are too close to us, because they blend into the field of what is familiar and a constant presence in our space.

Oftentimes, it is hard to differentiate between what we are used to and what is good for us; what we are used to is not always good for us. The only way to REALLY build in the ability to discern what behavior is acceptable from others (that is to challenge mistreatment by others), is to monitor how you treat yourself, and make any abusive or neglectful stance unwelcome. That way you will open a seeing eye on your blind spot, make what was hidden visible to your awareness. This will help you to challenge others automatically when they mistreat you, without a thought of self-doubt.

In other words: stop doing it to yourself, and that way you will stop attracting or allowing the same from others. Believe it or not, we create our own reality by the very way we treat ourselves. Think of it as qualities that we cultivate; each one of our thoughts, attitudes, and behaviors is an act of cultivation of that quality, of that energetic vibration. It will attract more of the same – that is just the way it works! You smile at yourself, they smile at you. You kick yourself, they kick you. You care, they care. What goes around inside of you, comes around into your life.

Of course, the cycle then continues: you give it to others, and they give it back to you; and it would be a futile exercise to look for who started it. Human interaction is circular, every stance and word is both a cause and an effect. The only way to heal a painful dynamic is to look inward, notice the "glitch" in your relationship to your own Self, and fix it. That way you will have the moral foundation to expect better from others.

Now you are tangled up in others,
And have forgotten what you once knew,
And that's why everything you do has some weird failure in it.
Kabir

Once you understand this, you will find that there is a profound implication here: blaming others, focusing on other people, things, events, authorities, etc. will distract you from taking charge of the only thing you can actually do: helping yourself. This external focus is what gets people stuck in old, yucky patterns of feeling, thinking and acting. Others cannot be responsible for your well-being, no matter how much they love and know you. This is because they do not have access to the necessary information: they do not know how you feel right now. Your job is to make sure that *you* do!

The way to be well is to practice shifting your focus from external to the internal, to the way you feel at any given point in time - like for instance, right now! How is your body feeling? Keep scanning your body for sensations all day long; that is where feelings live. Paying attention to how you feel *right now* will set you on the road to self-help – the only help that is always available, right where you are, right in this moment.

Relationships as Mirrors

A loving person lives in a loving world.
A hostile person lives in a hostile world.
Everyone you meet is your mirror.
Ken Keyes

As above, so below: what's true on a small scale is also true on a large scale. We cannot overstep our shadow, we are poised to re-create our reality, over and over: if you ignore your feelings, others will also neglect you; if you abuse or disrespect yourself – your body or your mind - others will hurt you, too.

We can't help but cultivate in our relationships the very same qualities we already have "at home" with our Selves. By and large it is safe to say that *the quality of our relationships is an extension, or a mirror image of how we treat ourselves.* Our self-parenting style will seep into and color our lives - for better or worse – with the energies it carries. You may not be able to change your outside relationships into positive ones single-handedly – it takes two to tango – but you are *always* able to change your relationship to yourself; this is what ultimately matters the most, anyway!

Are you unaware of your feelings? Neglectful to yourself in ANY way? Do you ignore your body's healthy needs for adequate (that means healthy and not too much or too little) food, enough rest, sleep or anything else? In response you will find yourself (i.e. your Inner Child) shut down, sleep too much, become depressed, sad, anxious, withdrawn and isolated.

You will also find the same patterns in your primary relationships (with lovers, partners, friends, spouses): you will feel neglected and lonely, not getting your needs met. When this happens, we typically blame the other for it, while we are practicing this same style in our treatment of our selves!

When we abuse ourselves emotionally or physically we find that others do the same to us. Do you feel criticized, blamed, shamed, or judged by others? This is because the inner pattern acts as a precedent, it unavoidably seeps into our outer patterns. It is true that it came from others in the first place, but once we grow up we typically re-create the same kind of environment for ourselves, the one we feel familiar with. In reality we collude with the abuse, because it blends in with our reality: we actually believe that it is normal. Then we perpetuate the hurt by pointing the fingers to those around us.

While the enemy of your own anger is unsubdued,
though you conquer external foes, they will only increase.
Togmay Zangpo

As we change the arrangement in our relationship with our own Selves, within, then will we have the awareness, perspective and motivation to change it without. Then we will be able to speak up and advocate for our true needs in a way that can and will be heard!

If you are nice to yourself, the world will follow suit. Don't believe it? Run an experiment. For the next one week listen to how you really feel, accept it, and speak your truth. Also, do not put yourself down in any way! You do this, and see what happens: I bet you my bottom dollar that those outside abusers and neglecters will start to fade out. Why? Because they are simply mirror images of your relationship to your own Self. Don't get mad at the mirror, just use it to learn.

I realize that in some places in the world, or some situations in our lifetimes it is harder to focus inward, due to the hurtful nature of the environment. If you find yourself in a culture, political environment, work place, family, or relationship that is abusive or neglectful, that does not know how to accept, appreciate or love it becomes an actual *mandate* to practice self-love. This will bring about healing on multiple levels: you will feel better because you are summoning your inner ally when you desperately need him; also, your environment will start healing, because this is how all change begins: small.

Not only that, also the energy, the example of your self-love practices will unavoidably trickle over into the environment, and thus, not only will you not contribute to the sick pattern, you will do your share in changing it. I am not saying "turn the other cheek". I am saying that you can practice attention, self-soothing, positive self-talk, and assertiveness in any situation, even if just between you and you. Do it, and watch what happens!

Now, granted that there are mean people in the world, try to look at the following chart as if it were a mirror for you to get a glimpse of your relationship to *yourself*. If you have mostly positive relationships, you are probably good to yourself. Too many (more than half) Neutral/Absents mean you may be absent from yourself, which translates into a pattern of self-neglect. Too many mean relationships means an overall negative relationship to ourselves, or self-abuse on some level.

Check the appropriate space for the overall quality of the following relationships:

	Friendly/Loving	Neutral/Absent	Unfriendly/Mean
Mother			
Father			
Brother 1, 2, 3			
Sister 1, 2, 3			
Friend 1, 2, 3			
Boss 1, 2			
Colleague 1, 2, 3			
The World in General			

My Honest Reader, see your reflection in the mirror of your relationships, and bless each image for the truths it brings you - they open the door for a healthy change!

Your Self-Parenting Style

Self-love, my liege, is not so vile a sin, as self-neglecting.
Shakespeare, Henry V.

You know, I find it funny how Nature "rears" us, in a real no-nonsense way. We get nourished with everything we need: air, water, food, sun. However, there are strict limits imposed on us as well: as soon as we don't listen, and behave in discord and disconnect with how we really feel, we get a consequence: we get "grounded", depressed or anxious, and unable to do what we should or want to do. Mother Nature strips us of our most valued and indispensable assets: energy, peace, focus, motivation. We only get them back once we have proven – not just promised! – that we *will* pay attention and listen to our Inner Child's voice...until the next time we don't.

Self-parenting is truly the key to a healthy life. Suffering, unhappiness, loss of balance in any way are symptoms of something going wrong in our most basic relationship, the one to our Selves. Typically, as we grow up we parent ourselves the same way we were raised. Not only will we treat ourselves the way we were treated, we also treat others the same way. Every relationship is parenting. If our self-parenting style is tainted with abuse or neglect on any level, this will seep into our relationships and contaminate them, thus making them less safe. Safety in intimacy is what we all need. We crave closeness, and often we don't know how to make it safe, so we can have and keep it.

There has been research at Harvard University on what makes for effective, positive parenting (Maccoby and Martin, 1983). They compared four criteria to see what combination would make for the best parenting: responsive vs. unresponsive and demanding vs. undemanding. I find these terms a little heavy and academic, so I am replacing them with more common terms that mean the same: warm vs. cold and restrictive vs. permissive. Warm and cold refer to the amount and quality of love that is expressed toward the child, and restrictive and permissive refer to the amount of limit-setting that the parents use in disciplining the child.

The style we use to parent ourselves is simply the cornerstone of one's well-being: it defines our health on every level. A wound that is cared for will heal – and so do we.

We choose our style of self-parenting without a thought, unconsciously, basically by following our role models- OR doing the opposite, as a reaction to our experience. If your parents were loving and warm, and set good boundaries and limitations on you, chances are you are faring pretty well in life. Love and limits are what respectively feed and keep us safe. However, there is a continuum of parenting styles, according to expressed love, or temperature, and the level of limit setting, or grip.

It is useful to measure parenting styles along these two factors, because Expressed Love directly translates into the degree the child feels loved, and Limit Setting spells the degree of safety the child experiences. Love and safety are the most fundamental ingredients of parenting in particular, and of any relationship, in general.

So what do these measures mean? Here is a rundown:

Expressed Love: love is kindness, positive attention, physical and verbal affection, affection, and care. It can be measured by "temperature", like this:

Hot:
Anger, threats, unpredictability, violence, verbal abuse, intrusiveness, emotional blackmail, guilt trips, mind games, physical or verbal inappropriateness, or sexual abuse, emotional incest (e.g. flirting with a child);

Warm:
Loving, kind, accepting, demonstrative, attentive, affectionate; at times "parentification" of a child (putting the child in a parent's role);

Cold:
Uncaring, emotionally or physically absent, neglectful, indifferent, disengaged, ignoring, abandoning, unaffectionate, unavailable.

We have two extremes here: hot can be loaded, scalding, like anger and unpredictability. It is not loving; even though there may be love, it is expressed inappropriately, and thus tainted with stress or negativity. Cold, on the other end, especially when on the sub-zero side, is the recommended temperature for killing any living organism. It is neglectful, and it really spells abandonment, thus it is not conducive to thriving. In such an environment the child does not feel loved, because love is not expressed neither in words, nor in actions, or behaviors.

On the temperature continuum the only environment for kids to thrive in a family is warm, a synonym for directly expressed acceptance, love, validation, attention, and the like.

Oneself, indeed, is one's own protector.
What other protector could there be?
With self-control
One gains a protector hard to obtain.
The Dhammapada

<u>Limit Setting</u>: Limits are necessary for the safety and health of a child. I measure it in the strength of the "grip" a parent uses to control the child. Too much is too much, of course, and too little is insufficient for the child to thrive physically and/or emotionally.

Domineering:
Critical, judgmental, blameful, intrusive, "my way, or the highway";

Restrictive:
Appropriate rules regarding health, safety, honesty, cooperation, etc., structure, chores, expects safe behaviors, consistent, reasonable discipline, enforces rules appropriately;

Permissive:
No rules, no consequences, inconsistent, allows child to rule the house, physically and/or emotionally neglectful.

A domineering parent would be abusive, emotionally, mentally, physically, or even sexually. A permissive parent on the other hand would be too lackadaisical (ignoring the child, being absent physically and/or emotionally) where there are too few limits for the child's good, in a way that would feel and be neglectful. The extreme end of this scale is abandonment. On the Limit Setting continuum the best parenting practice is Restrictive, because it translates into teaching and enforcing the rules of safety, health and cooperation. This is the style where kids feel safe, knowing they can rely on their elders for guidance. Safety in intimacy – wow, what a gift!

Granted, in a two parent family usually there are two different parenting styles, unless they add up to a warm and restrictive environment, the child will learn a style of self-parenting that will cause problems in his life. Truth be told, even if the parents did not have what it took to offer a warm and restrictive environment, as long as there was a close relative or adult who could, this can make all the difference for the child's life. Any combination will lead to the child adopting that style for himself – or, in extreme cases do the exact opposite, usually another extreme (e.g. a domineering style can lead to overly permissive self-parenting, with lack of basic discipline for health and safety). The good news is that self-parenting styles can be corrected later in life!

The hot/domineering style is common in families where the collective is more important than the individual's needs, e.g. where there is a parent with chronic illness, or substance abuse, or in traditional societies with a clan-type family structure (e.g. Southern Europe, Middle East). Within such societies this style is the norm, therefore it is not necessarily experienced by children as abusive. The rules are unreasonably strict, the consequences harsh. In the context of a Western society, however, kids who are brought up in families employing this style of parenting are considered abused, physically, emotionally, at times even sexually, and grow up "walking on eggshells", fearful of life – or, conversely, to be aggressors themselves. This style spells negative attention and communication, lack of acceptance or validation, lack of safety and soothing, and emotional unavailability.

The hot/restrictive style is some combination of anger or intrusiveness, with the safety of reliable rules, expectations, consistency and structure. This style produces negative attention, lack of validation, negative communication, in combination with a measure of safety due to the restrictiveness.

The hot/permissive style is known for flying tempers, intrusiveness, qualities that convey negative attention, combined with a quality of lack of attention, i.e. neglect. The child is left hurt, lost and confused. The environment is emotionally, or even physically unsafe, abusive, while also neglectful of the child's needs.

The warm/domineering style provides love and care, but at the cost of having to be very obedient and quiet. Depending on the degree of abusiveness the child may come out pretty intact, with just some bruised confidence and self-esteem, or, on the other extreme, unable to make decisions for himself, afraid of, and constantly deferring back to the parent.

The warm/restrictive style (even if it is the result of a combo from elements of the two parents' styles) is the only one where the child feels truly safe and well. Love is a necessary, but not sufficient component of a child's well-being; safety is the other. He must feel that there are reasonable rules, and that different behaviors will result in rewards, or consequences. Overall this style of parenting is effective, because the parents offer love and nourishment in all ways, while surrounding the child with effective limits for health and safety. This would look like "yes, you may have another piece of chocolate" (or have your friends over, etc.), and "no, you may not stay up late on a school night" (or smoke pot, or drink, or run in front of a bus).

The warm/permissive style would translate into children feeling loved but neglected. Often, they feel their parents are more like pals than authority figures, therefore there are not enough limits set. Sometimes, kids in a warm/permissive family are "parentified", that is they are made to be the parent's parent (these are the kids who have to take care of younger siblings, or be a parent's confidants). This makes a child feel uneasy insecure, or overwhelmed, because kids know that they don't know the answers, or have the maturity, or the skills to keep themselves (let alone others!) safe and well. The resulting discomfort makes a child either completely self-reliant, unable to trust and involve others, or depressed, wanting to push the limits in order to somehow elicit them, hoping to *then* feel safe and secure. In my clinical experience many people with a drug addiction grew up with this primary parenting style. Therefore, as adults they cannot set limits to themselves, and indulge in at least one thing, preferably something strongly forbidden or outrageous, and thus provoking the parent - or the law - to step in and set a firm limit.

The cold/domineering style of parenting spells neglect *and* abuse, both of the "evil twins", exposing the child to the worst conditions for thriving. In extreme cases some kids living in this type of environment actually fail to thrive, are emaciated, and do not grow appropriately. Kids from such an environment grow up feeling invisible, unimportant, unloved, often depressed, and unable to be good parents themselves. No expressed love, coupled with high expectations (lots of chores, plenty of "NO!"'s, strong rules, no permission to express feelings, or demands for the highest grades) is an unfair deal. There is more give than receive, so kids feel shortchanged, unloved, taken for granted or even advantage of.

The cold/restrictive style of parenting feels emotionally neglectful, while somewhat caring to children. Restrictiveness has many shades of grey, and used appropriately it is necessary in child rearing: since there are limits, the implication is that there is "someone home", holding down the fort. That is comforting for a child, because it manifests attention to their safety and well-being, and offers some structure to their lives. However, there is more give than take in this equation, where the child is expected to "behave" but receives no rewards for being good.

The cold/permissive style of parenting is an environment where the child will feel unloved and neglected, like he is on his own in the world. This style means no attention being paid to the child, akin to the way it feels to be an orphan, only worse, because with at least one parent in the picture the lack of love and limits sticks out as a sore thumb. Kids are left feeling invisible, unimportant and alone.

This is how children grow up to treat (i.e. parent) themselves in adulthood just the way they were parented. The amount of abuse or neglect present in our upbringing will define our level of adjustment in adulthood. Our parents' style becomes our self-parenting style. You hurt me, I hurt me. You ignore me, I ignore me. You violate me, I violate me. You love me, I love me. You discipline me, I discipline me. The only exception in continuing on the same self-parenting mode is when the parent's style is extreme, it is way too harsh, or way too neglectful. Extreme harshness or restrictiveness may lead to over-indulgence in self-parenting, letting oneself eat, drink, sleep, or hang out too much (i.e. neglect), while extreme neglect may result in the other pole, the person over-achieving, or micromanaging his life (i.e. abuse).

A person who grew up with a pattern of abuse of neglect is what we call a traumatized person. You can feel traumatized not just by a discreet painful event, but also by a painful, long-standing condition. Of course, there is trauma, too, very often not inflicted on the child by a parent, but others (examples include bullying, physical or verbal abuse, molestation, accidents, etc.). Until it is resolved, trauma will have a powerful effect on someone's self-parenting; it will throw you off-track until it is effectively treated. For the majority of people we blindly bring our parents' attitudes and practices along into our adulthood both in our treatment of ourselves, and of our kids - until further notice!

Indeed, if the record needs to be corrected, it can, and must be corrected. Parents are only vehicles to teach us how to treat ourselves for the rest of our lives to be well. They took their turn, and did their best, for sure. Game is not over, though. Now, it's the second round: we get to choose how we will parent ourselves, by learning the skills involved. Now, YOU ARE THE BOSS!

My dear Reader, this is that further notice! If you don't feel happy in your life, you do not have to treat yourself the way you were treated. You can learn right here how to change your self-parenting style - and when you do, health, peace and balance will follow closely!

Parenting Styles

How Were You Raised?

Expressed Love	+	Limit Setting	=	Parenting Style
Hot	+	Domineering	=	Abusive/Abusive
Hot	+	Restrictive	=	Abusive/Caring
Hot	+	Permissive	=	Abusive/Neglectful
Warm	+	Domineering	=	Caring/Abusive
Warm	**+**	**Restrictive**	**=**	**Caring/Caring**
Warm	+	Permissive.	=	Caring/Neglectful
Cold/Gelid	+	Domineering	=	Neglectful/Abusive
Cold/Gelid	+	Restrictive	=	Neglectful/Caring
Cold/Gelid	+	Permissive	=	Neglectful/Neglectful

Using this scale there is a number of different combinations, only one of which – warm and restrictive - is truly healthy parenting. Short of extremes by either parent, the child may end up faring pretty well, as long as the different caretakers bring in these two qualities and thus complement each other's parenting style.

What is your self-parenting style at the present moment? Here is a questionnaire. Answer the questions, and find out what type of self-parenting you have been using:

Self-Parenting Questionnaire

LOVE

1.	Do you love yourself?	Y	N
2.	Do you like yourself?	Y	N
3.	Are you usually aware of your feelings?	Y	N
4.	Do you pay attention to your physical body?	Y	N
5.	Do you trust your body's signals?	Y	N
6.	Do you speak kindly to yourself?	Y	N

7. Do you usually know what you need to be well?   Y   N
8. Do you give yourself what you need?   Y   N
9. Do you get along with the people closest to you?   Y   N
10. Are you available for the people closest to you?   Y   N
11. Do you accept your feelings or needs?   Y   N
12. Are your thoughts mostly positive?   Y   N

The more "yes" answers you have the better you are doing in giving yourself the love you need and deserve. Conversely, the more you answered "no" the more likely you are to be reactive (abusive or neglectful) in your self-parenting.

LIMIT SETTING

1. Is your body free of aches and pains?   Y   N
2. Do you feel happy and energized most of the time?   Y   N
3. Are you free from addictions?   Y   N
4. Are you free from compulsions to shop, gamble, use porn, the internet, gaming, exercising?   Y   N
5. Are you disciplined regarding your health/safety?   Y   N
6. Do you exercise   Y   N
7. Do you work 8 hours or less a day?   Y   N
8. Do you eat junk food more than once a week?   Y   N
9. Is your food intake reasonable? (not too much or too little)   Y   N
10. Do you limit negative company?   Y   N
11. Do you get enough sleep (7-10 hours)?   Y   N
12. Do you feel emotionally and physically safe?   Y   N

The more "yes" answers you have the better you are doing in giving yourself the limits you need. Conversely, the more you answered "no" the more likely you are to be reactive (abusive or neglectful) in your self-parenting.

By now I can almost hear you say "alright, enough already, I get it, what's next? *How* do I do this?" Funny you should ask, I was going to tell you that right now!

PART FIVE

Your Steps to Self-Parenting with Love

As we develop a sense of Self, our intuitive voice becomes our natural and constant source of guidance... Self-understanding and acceptance, the bond we form with ourselves, is in many ways the most crucial spiritual challenge we face.

Carolyne Myss

Imagine a loudspeaker, announcing in a solemn voice:

"You are the one and only person responsible for your well-being. You were given this life to safeguard it, cherish it, enjoy it, and to make sure you are well, so you may perform what you were born to do: to fully realize yourself, and evolve."

The four practical steps to build and maintain happiness consist of the A-B-C-D practices; they provide a set of skills that will help you to *respond*, rather than *react* to your own stress. Stress reactions of abusing or neglecting one's Self under duress are not appropriate for our human experience, because living in society any given stress on any given day is not a matter of life or death. Barring extreme circumstances chances are we shall survive sitting in traffic, or feeling hurt by someone's words or attitude. For thriving - as opposed to surviving – you will need skills that will help you respond, rather than react to the stress within or without you. When you are responsive to your own stress, you are giving yourself love. Love heals, and not by magic: it heals by offering up loving care to the pain of the Self or Others.

Care is made of the four distinct practices in the acronym A-B-C-D. This sequence is a set of (self-)care skills, simplified, organized and streamlined for ease of use. It contains the four most fundamental practices that constitute health on every possible level. None of these practices can be omitted, or skipped over, or skimped because there is no fat to be found in this system. It is as lean as they come. Learn it and practice it, and you will be healed and transformed – along with your whole life!

I have heard people say that they are worried that if they used these new skills they will change, and not be able to recognize themselves anymore. In other words, they fear losing their identity. If your identity is that of suffering, I would say yes, go ahead and lose it! Otherwise, you are a lot more than anything you think or do. Using wholesome self-care will just bring out the best version of you: present, caring, positive, and, above all well. You are not to protect yourself from a change that can bring the things you need the most.

It is now time to shed the old fears and the behaviors, and the feelings and thoughts that came along with them. Can you see that they do not work anymore? And that is because the situation changed: you do not depend on anyone, you are all grown up, strong, capable and resourceful. What you learned you can unlearn and relearn.

Let us reiterate the four practices involved; they form an upward cycle of health, a chain, where each step builds on the previous one, and brings it forth to resolution. Remember, the goal is to feel better, and better, and even better. There is *always* better!

A is for Attention to physical sensations in your body, so you may be Aware, and Accept them as the truth of how you are feeling at this very moment. We will practice scanning the body for sensations, and then, we shall

B, Breathe into the most intense sensation, because by now we know that it is truthful, compacted information about how you feel and what you need. In order to read this coded information we must breathe into it, so as to be able to linger with the sensation, rather than react to it (by shutting down, or attacking it with judgment). Now that we are being soothed by the breaths (and a few other methods), we can proceed to

C, Communicate with the sensation about the truth of how we are feeling, and what we need to feel better, so that we may

D, Do just that! Once we have done what the body said, (or Deliver to our own needs) we will notice that the original sensation has lessened, if not dissipated altogether. This means we have effectively given ourselves what we needed, therefore we feel better.

As you practice **A-B-C-D** in your relationship with yourself you are not just healing that. You are also learning the skills to make all your relationships work. Paying attention (**A**) to the other, accepting their feelings and needs, and then (**B**) soothing the other and the interactions (de-escalate), and (**C**) communicating with the other about each person's feelings and needs, and then actually (**D**) doing what you agreed upon will lead to cooperation and the healing of any relationship. Do try this at home!

The A-B-C-D sequence forms an upward spiral of ever improving self-care, resulting in health, balance, and joy.

In the following I will lead you through these exercises. As you perform them, please watch which ones are difficult for you: where are you getting stuck? This is very important to notice, because each step is built on the previous one, and consequently is an integral part of the whole process. The stage or step that causes you the most difficulty will be the one that will need the most attention and practice on your part; slow down there, practice the skills that will help you un-do any obstacles in the your way to parent yourself positively. As you do that, shortly you will be able to whisk through all four steps in no time, anywhere, anytime; in other words, you will never be alone. *The goal is for you to be able to perform all four steps, automatically, throughout the day, every day and in every segment of your life.*

These four steps will help you to identify what you can do to feel better, and exactly when. So imagine you are going through the day, and you are noticing one (or more) of the following:

1. You are not feeling well (physically or emotionally)
2. Something unpleasant is happening.
3. You are saying something negative to yourself

As soon as you notice, ask yourself:

- "Am I aware of how my body- or my heart - feels? Am I accepting it as the truth? (A);
- Am I breathing / soothing myself with it? (B);
- Am I communicating with it about my feelings and my needs? I;
- Am I doing what it says? (D).

This framework will help you to lock in on what *you* can do.

Each of these steps represents a quality that is indispensable for well-being and peace. Since each of them is equally necessary *do not skip over any one step*! We all have a tendency to automatically avoid the steps that don't come easy. But remember: these are the very ones you need the most!

If you find that one of the four steps is more of a challenge you will find more exercises, as well as readings that will help to dissolve any stuck-ness in the Appendix. (If you are still having difficulty a good therapist could help dissolve any trauma that is keeping you stuck. Do not put up with anything less!)

As you continue to do your A-B-C-D's you will start feeling better and better each day. Do not stop using this method when you feel better, however! It is the medicine that keeps on giving, but only as long as you take it. Build it into your system as an automatic mechanism because it is the healthiest of habits.

How to Use the A-B-C-D Exercises

In the following part of this book you will find the exercises involved in each of the steps. The ones presented in the main text are the most essential ones – and you will find more in the Appendix. I suggest you read the chapter, and when you get to an exercise simply put the book aside and try it.

The exercises are designed to build the skills to be able to perform the four steps continuously, throughout the day, automatically. This mechanism will come in handy especially when you are not feeling great, or before making a decision, or committing to a course of action. In order to have these skills readily available it is important that you practice them *outside* of the context of these situations; it is much easier to learn them this way, than trying to practice something when you are already in the throes of stress.

I find it helps to designate a specific time of the day to practice all four steps, whenever you can take twenty minutes of peace and quiet, without interruptions. Unplug your electronics, they will not go bad! As you develop more ease, it will take you less and less time to do this, until you will be able to go through the whole protocol in a matter of seconds, even. Feel free to do it as often as possible, because the goal is for this to become your second nature. If you build up your skills like this, they will become your automatic pilot, and serve you instantaneously when you need them; you can just pull them out of your hat of tricks, so to speak, as the need arises. Think of it as basic training for health!

Preparing the foundation: Meet your Inner Child

In order to become the best possible parent to your Self you must forge a fundamental bond with your inner Self, or your Inner Child. The following exercise is indispensable because it will serve a few fundamental purposes:

- it will help you to direct positive emotion – i.e. love, attention, and acceptance – toward yourself (for some people this is may be a first!);
- it will make your Inner Child the center of your universe, and the first priority on your list; and
- it will also help you create a basic covenant between your Inner Parent and your Inner Child, a working contract of sorts, where your adult Self commits to take care of your child Self.

Therefore, the following exercise lays the foundation for any good self-parenting in the future. However, meeting your Inner Child can feel like a real challenge.

If that is the way you feel, or if you find yourself avoiding this exercise, do not fret, stay, and try to make it more comfortable to do this, a sort of ritual that feels nourishing and soothing: light a candle, dim the lights, put on some relaxing music, and get started.

First, find a childhood picture of yourself, one you can relate to, and love, and commit to paying attention to. Take a close look at that picture, and see the cute and loveable younger you, the innocent child, who is expecting only the best out of life.

1. Close your eyes, plant your feet on the ground and unfold your hands, fingers and legs. Pay attention to the sensations on the soles of your feet, and the way they connect you to the <u>ground</u>, and the Earth beneath them.

2. Now, imagine yourself in a <u>safe place</u>, like a beach, or a mountaintop. Pretend you are actually there right now: see the sights...smell the air... feel the sensations on your skin...hear the sounds...and really, really feel, experience the safety, the comfort and the peace this place brings you. Feel it in your bones...and

3. As you sit there, <u>see your younger Self</u>, the one in the picture, approaching you from a distance. Let him or her come closer, and closer to you, and then let this younger Self of yours sit right by you, or even in your lap. Hold this child in your arms, and soothe this child, tell him or her something along the lines of the following:

4. *"<u>You are the apple of my eye</u>...you are beautiful inside and out, just a perfect little being, and I love you with all my heart. You are my first born child, and from now on I will always pay attention to you, and take care of you BETTER THAN ANYONE EVER did! I will listen to you, and believe you, and I will give you what you need, because you deserve all the care in the world! I will keep you safe from harm. I am so sorry that I was absent from you. You will never again be alone, I will always be here for you! I promise you that I will NOW*

learn how to take care of you. I love you so very much!" Make this a solemn vow, a sacred promise that carries all the emotional impact you can muster. Really mean it.

5. Continue talking to your younger Self until he or she stops squirming, is calm and is believing your words. You will *know* when you can <u>feel the connection</u> to your younger Self.

6. When ready, shrink this child down to the size of your heart, and <u>place it into your heart</u>, into the coziest corner, where he or she will stay forever...close enough to your ears so you will hear it when she or he calls on you. <u>Promise this child you will listen to your body</u> from now on, and trust its signals, because you know it is your truthful younger Self, calling for you!

At this time, in order to firm up this inner connection you may also want to write a letter to your Inner Child, speaking to him/her in a loving, kind, compassionate tone, the one you would use with someone you adore, and who depends on you for everything. Giving your commitment for a strong, connected relationship with your Younger Self in writing makes this a sacred contract of sorts that staples your intention into your subconscious. When you are done with the letter date it, and sign it to make this a truly spiritually binding contract.

FIRST STEP: A: Attention, Acceptance

GOAL: To pay attention to your body, notice and accept the way you feel throughout the day.

The throbbing vein

Will take you further

Than any thinking.

Muhammad said, "Don't theorize

About essence!" All speculations

Are just more layers of covering.

Human beings love coverings!

They think the designs on the curtains

Are what's being concealed.

Rumi

Attention

Attention is like sunshine: it is one of the most fundamental needs. It says you have a right to exist.

> *An old joke: The old shopkeeper is dying; his whole family gathers around him, and with his eyes closed he inquires, "Are you here, my wife Anne?" "Yes, dear", she replies, "And are you here, my son John?", "Yes, Father", "And are you here, my son Erin?" "Yes, Father", "And you, my daughter Cathy?, "Yes, Father", at which point the old man startles, sits up, and yells out, "Then, who is tending the shop??"*

Is anybody home with *you*, tending to *your* metaphorical "shop"? I know, I know: paying attention to your body's sensations is easier said than done.

What if it hurts? What if I cannot help it? Worse yet, what if it gets worse? What if I burst, go crazy, get into trouble, hospitalized, jailed, or even die? These are pretty common fears about paying attention to one's Self. The gamut goes from trepidation to terror. Will you believe me if I say that *none* of this will happen? (If you are truly terrified, by all means, do this in the company of someone you trust). You will be safe, in fact, a lot safer than if you did not pay attention! What's the worst case scenario? You will cry, and run to someone for help. Remember, you are opening the door on your younger Self, inquiring about how he is feeling. From now on, he will not be home alone, orphaned, shivering abandoned in the dark.

Your body is not supposed to be without sensation, in fact, it is a sea of unending and ever-changing sensation. Make it a point to befriend the notion – and the experience – that intensity is part of a normal life. In fact, just because something that might have hurt you in the past felt intense, that does not make intensity the enemy, or something abnormal. Go with the flow of it, lean into it, learn to trust it: it knows better, and it will take you safely ashore, to the right place at the right time. Life has a knack for doing just that! So let go. Pretend you are in a movie theater watching your body's experiences as if it was a show. You don't have to jump in and rescue, just witness and feel.

When you are stressed and do not pay attention to how you feel you add insult to injury: not only are you in distress, you are also alone in it, the Inner Parent is gone, and the Inner Child is all alone and in trouble. Have compassion to yourself when you don't feel well, do not ignore your pain or discomfort on any level. Instead, pay attention, acknowledge, and accept it. "A"-it! It is the only way to be able to help yourself: you can only help what you know about.

In order to develop the "witness stance" (the way it is called in yoga), that is to pay attention to your body's sensations – or "felt sense" – you will need to silence and bridle your mind first. Mind chatter is a formidable distraction from what is. Reel your thoughts back into your body, from its wanderings on past or future events, or other times, people and things. Bring them back into a single focus, which is the opposite of scattered. It is like de-cluttering a room; throw out what you don't need, basically most of what you have there, so you can use your room/mind-space to be, to feel.

When the witness is aware,
The lake of mind is still,
And in that mirrored surface
I see my own true face
As Spirit smiling back at me.
Danna Faulds

Exercise 1. Breathing

Your first and foremost self-help tool is your breath. Focus only on your breath, and make your exhales slower than your inhales; this will relax your body and your mind. Let's start.

1. Breathe in to the slow count of six, ready? ...One...two...three...four... five...six...
2. hold it on the top for a second, and then
3. Release it, slowly, to the count of seven ...one...two...three...four... five...six...seven.
4. Now, repeat three more times.

Do you feel calmer? You have just triggered the relaxation response in your body, the one that activates your parasympathetic nervous system responsible for calming. Train yourself to instantaneously start to breath slowly as you are beginning to get stressed, like ... always! Often people stop breathing under stress, so go against your first reaction, because it is a reaction – just like the bug freezing when feeling threatened. Unless we breathe, we freeze and cannot respond adequately to the constant flux of inner or outer stress. Breath de-escalates, relaxes your muscles, and focuses your mind on the breathing; you just cannot do any better than that! Through breath, you are tuning in with yourself, staying present and calming, instead of taking flight from your feelings, thus abandoning yourself in the midst of the stress.

If you have too many thoughts buzzing in your mind it will help to think of them as bored children. Given them something to play with, to fascinate over. This could be anything, a sound, a flower, a word, that in meditation we call a mantra. But I find that the most helpful single focus for the mind is your body. Not only will this type of focusing help you to tap into your body's information about your feelings and needs, it will also relax you at the same time. Make your awareness linger on the sensations in your body – and be fascinated by them! Be a witness to what is. You can learn to hone your ability to focus; it is a simple skill, and with daily practice, within a week or so you will be very proficient.

There are many ways to silence the mind – and believe it or not, you are the boss of your mind, and not the other way around.

Exercise 2. : Switching off the Mind

1. Sit quietly, relax your body and take a few deep breaths.
2. Imagine opening the door to your mind; enter it, and look for the lever, switch, or handle that controls your mind chatter. It might even say "Mind Chatter" on it.
3. When you found it, switch it off, and let yourself experience the ensuing silence. Take your time doing this, and do not stop until you have found the switch and shut it off completely.

OR, Exercise 3. Balloon Technique

1. Rate your mind-chatter 0 to 10 (lowest to highest).
2. Sit quietly, relax your body and take a few deep breaths.
3. Imagine a helium balloon – see the size, shape, and color, maybe even smell it...
4. Allow your first thought, worry or anxiety to emerge
5. Lock it into the balloon...
6. ...and now, let go of that balloon...see it fly up and up, into the sky.
7. Now imagine another helium balloon...see the color, size, shape...
8. Allow your next thought, worry, or anxiety to come up...
9. Lock it into that balloon...and ready? Let go of that balloon also...see it fly all the way up, and up, until it disappears.
10. Continue with more balloons until your mind is clear. Take your time.
11. Rate your mind-chatter again, from 0 to 10 to see how well this exercise worked for you.

At this point your mind is clear, and you are ready to focus on your body. In fact, use that focus *now* to pay attention to the soles of your feet.

When I soften, release and breathe,
I discover I am more than
What I think, feel, reason, or believe.
Dana Faulds

Exercise 4. Grounding

1. Notice the place where your feet touch the ground, that surface where you are connected to the rest of the physical World.

    Feel the sensations generating... you may notice some warmth, heaviness, or tingling on the soles of your feet. Make that interface come alive with your attention.

2. Now, let your feet sink an inch or two into the moist soil, and then sprout some strong, sturdy roots down into the Earth from your feet... creating an organic connection with the Earth beneath your feet, as if you were a strong tree... Let your roots grow as long and wide as they need to for a firm grip into the soil, for stability, and nourishment.

3. To the count of six slowly inhale comfort and peace from the Earth through your roots, up into your heart...let your heart soak those feelings up...

4. Slowly exhale any leftovers down through your feet into your roots, and then into the ground.

5. Repeat three times.

By now, you should feel nice and relaxed, present, and able to tune in with your body for information and guidance about how to take care of yourself right now. First, let us find the sensations present in the body in this very moment. This is the source of all information, the one we don't want to shut down or ignore, because that would be tantamount to shooting the messenger. The body talks, and no information there is superfluous, or random. For now, just trust that it *knows something you do not* (even if you think you do!).

NOTE: If your body is producing a very noticeable sensation as we speak, for instance if you have a splitting headache, you can skip the Body Scanning, since you already know where you feel and what. Go to the form below and write down this information in the first two columns. Then, jump to Exercise 6 (Accepting Self-Talk).

Before you start this exercise read the List of Body Sensations, to have a clear idea for what you are looking for.

Achy	Flowing	Queasy
Bloated	Fluttery	Quivery
Blocked	Fragile	Radiating
Breathless	Frantic	Restricted
Calm	Frozen	Raw
Clammy	Full	Shaky
Cold	Fuzzy	Sharp
Cool	Heavy	Smooth
Congested	Heated	Spacey
Constricted	Hollow	Spacious
Contracted	Hot	Spinning
Damp	Inflated	Still
Deflated	Itchy	Strong
Disconnected	Jittery	Suffocating
Dry	Jumpy	Sweaty
Dull	Knotted	Tense
Dizzy	Light	Thick
Electric	Nervous	Thin
Empty	Numb	Tight
Energized	Paralyzed	Tingly
Expanded	Pounding	Trembling
Expansive	Pressure	Throbbing
Faint	Prickly	Twitchy
Flaccid	Puffy	Warm
Floating	Pulsing	Wobbly

By Susan A. Purnell, SoulAliveWomen.com

Exercise 5. Body Scanning

1. Switch off your mind. You are like a scientist in the lab, simply noticing what is, without any judgment, opinion or interpretation.

2. Using your mind as a sharp, sophisticated scanner, let it pick up sensation in your body... anywhere... any kind of sensation

3. Start scanning from the top of your head...
   - Your face...
   - Your front
   - Sides of your head... taking notes of any sensation you may find, without thinking...
   - Scan your eyes (any wetness, dryness, heaviness, etc.)
   - Your mouth...
   - Your jaws...
   - Scanning your neck now... the sides of your neck, back of your neck
   - Scanning your throat (any soreness, dryness, pressure, or lump?)
   - Scanning your shoulders, taking notes...
   - Scanning your upper back...
   - Your middle back...
   - And your lower back...
   - Scanning your arms, upper, elbows, lower arms...
   - Hands and fingers.
   - Now, scanning your chest area... any sensation there (pressure, choppy or shallow breath, etc.)?
   - Checking in with your heart, any ache, clenching, or any other sensation?
   - Check in with your belly now, any pressure, tension, or butterflies? Take notes as you go...
   - Scanning your hips,
   - Your thighs,

- Your knees...
- Scanning your lower legs, calves and shins...
- All the way down to your feet and your toes.
- And now, scan your whole body to see if there is any feeling, energy or sensation you are carrying in your whole body?

4. Take the following Authenticity Process Sheet (or make a copy of it) and simply write down whatever came up, the location under "Where in the body", and the sensation under, well, "Sensation". You can use the same sheet to record information for all the following steps as well.

Yudit Maros

Authenticity Process Sheet

A Where in Body	A Sensations What	B Intensity 1-10	C Feelings 5x	C Needs 5x	D WWWHHH
(E.g. Head	Ache	5	Sadness	Talk to Mom	Tonight

Let your attention zero in on the most intense sensation in your body. Where is it? What is it? How intense is it from 1 to 10 (from mildest to strongest)? Plug this information into the first three columns of the table above.

...And breathe...stay with it...it is only trying to inform you of something you might not know...something important.

Right now, this may look like a whole lot of work, but it is really a very simple matter of training the mind to pick up on sensation in real time. Soon, with practice (give it a week or so of daily scanning) you will get so good at this that you will be able to send a flash of attention through your body in a matter of seconds, and zero in on the part that carries the most sensation. If you can't find any sensation, you may not be picking up on the more subtle feelings in your body. Breathe, relax, focus, scan, and you will find them, even if they are just a nice warm feeling in the belly – so don't expect to find anything dramatic! This is all a matter of getting used to noticing and listening to very subtle signals, just like in a dream. If you do, you will be privy to fantastic depths and perspectives that provide the truest guidance.

Unless you have ease with noticing and accepting how you are feeling, the body's sensations are the easiest to notice and use for self-help. There are, however, other portals to the truth of your feelings: your emotions, thoughts, and behaviors– and of course, dreams. These are not as easy to detect, because often our awareness gets lost in our everyday thoughts or actions, but it helps to remember to watch out for these as well. Uncontrollable, racing thoughts? Outbursts of anger, anyone? Inability to move? Running around like a maniac? Choosing to do something that you don't feel like doing? Doing something *instead* of what would help you to feel better? Anything funky with your sleeping or eating? These are also messages from your inner Self to you that must be decoded. So do pay attention to what you are thinking, doing, how you are behaving, talking, and what you are choosing, because these are truthful reflections, in real-time of how you are feeling. If you are unable to find a sensation in your body use these as the gateway to the truth: consider them as important as a body sensation, and treat them as if they were signals from your system – which they are. *Catch the thought or behavior as it is occurring*, and ask yourself how you are feeling right now. From here, proceed to **A**cceptance, believing that there is no higher truth than yours, right here, right now.

> *Alice was in deep denial about her pill addiction, until she scanned her body and became aware of the unbearable anxiety she was feeling – something she was so used to, she never even noticed anymore. By scanning her body she realized that the anxiety was a symptom of her prescription drug abuse. This realization enabled her to admit to herself that there is a big problem, and accept the truth - and true weight - of it. This prompted her telling the truth to her doctor, and started her on the path of recovery. She said this awareness and acceptance of something she did not want or was not able to see quite possibly saved her life.*

Acceptance

You must accept your body sensations as Your Truth, something you do not get to choose, something you only get to cooperate with. The alternative is to get hurt, plain and simple. We do not have control over how our bodies feel in the first place. As a general rule, it is best to stay with the program Nature dictates, and keep our need to control at bay. What happens when we don't? We run up against a wall, expecting not to get hurt...hmm...I'll see if there is an opening in my schedule...

Now, does this mean everything is always to be accepted? No, but we are wise to limit our non-acceptance to the things, and circumstances that 1. we can change, and 2. are truly harmful to our safety or health. (Hint: a little discomfort never killed anybody!). As Reinhold Niebuhr put it most aptly in his now world-famous Serenity Prayer:

God grant me the serenity
To accept the things I cannot change;
Courage to change the things I can;
And the wisdom to know the difference.

Is the sacred "out there" or is it "in here?" I believe that Life's (God's, Nature's) intelligence, wisdom, love and guidance are all built into our own bodies – or energetic systems – to guide us. Do not look for it "out there". Have faith in your own Self, who carries all the intelligence of this awesome, sacred world. *This*, my friend, is faith in action, faith that Life takes care of us, that Nature knows her stuff, that we must not worry, but accept the truth of what is, and work with it. Nothing is truer than the way you feel this very moment, and it is the only guidance you have (take my word for it, I am a professional guide!). Another person's experience, or truth does not trump yours. You only have your own to work with – so do! *Pay attention, accept the way you feel; go from there, and you cannot go wrong.*

Since only *you* can access and read your own feelings, you are the only person you can truly help. Feelings are just that: temporary emotional states; they do not define who you are. Accept them as feelings, so you may help yourself to feel better. If you get "attached" to them, and identify with them, you are short-circuiting your ability to step outside of the feeling and help yourself.

> *Mary put it like this: "I felt like I was flawed. That I was made to be impatient and anxious. I thought that acceptance meant I just needed to work with those qualities and the people around me needed to deal with me as I was. I now realize that I can feel better, and acceptance is really the first part to becoming who I am meant to be: relaxed and patient".*

Is it bad to forgive, accept, and even rejoice in how you feel? I believe radical acceptance of yourself (as Tara Brach puts it) is actually the foundation for growing, and making changes in our behavior and outlook. We go to museums to admire the likeness – of who? Of ourselves. Why can't we look in the mirror and do the same? No matter what you do in the world, you must accept your feelings as the truth. Only if you do can you align your thoughts and actions with it, and then do what it takes to feel better. If you do not, you are failing at the only task you were assigned at birth: to take care of you. The people you consider bad are the ones who failed at this task, their energy derailed into destructive behaviors. If you need to work on forgiving yourself you will find an exercise for this in the Appendix.

> *Take a moment to admit to yourself, and accept the fact that*
> *you are fundamentally good enough <u>just the way you are</u>.*

I have decided to accept my own thoughts as the truth.

Georgia O'Keefe

My point is this: short of things clearly outrageous, immoral, exploitative, or evil we must learn to accept life the way it is, including our own selves. Use discernment in your discernment. If and when you truly do not like something in yourself, your life, your world, accept that you do not, and act accordingly, so there is no conflict within you. Accept how you feel, first, and foremost. Acceptance is a general stance, an attitude that provides the warm, nourishing environment for things, and people to flourish.

The only real wisdom is knowing you know nothing.

Socrates

Why is it essential to learn to accept one's own feelings? Because this is the very foundation of health. Acceptance is faith, trust in Life, in that the world provides, and that we are supposed to be here. Open yourself up to this, stop the blocking of the very energy that is supposed to nourish you. This foundational stance will ensure a steady flow of constant healing and replenishment that you could not do for yourself if you tried. This is why they say it is wise to not know. Forget your notions about how you should feel, and what is good for you. STOP! Listen to how you feel, and accept it, blindly.

If a man wishes to be sure of the road he treads on,
he must close his eyes and walk in the dark.

St. John of the Cross

Kate is a slight, spunky fifty something woman, sharp both in her looks and her intellect. She had been battling an insidious eating disorder, a combo of anorexia and bulimia for all her life. She has been denying herself food and other nourishment, like rest, sleep, time off, forever. After practicing A and B for a few weeks she came back with sparkling eyes and a big smile, saying that there has been a tremendous shift in her life: she is now letting herself be full, letting it be OK to feel good. She is not anxious anymore about her next meal. She said "My whole life has been about withholding nourishment, like love, food, nature, sun. I am learning to receive, to feed myself, and to be in balance. I am learning that I am not just a giver, a caretaker of others: that I can receive!"

The mere act of paying attention to her body without any judgment triggered this major change in Jill's life and health. This is because **A**, i.e. positive

Attention *is* Acceptance, the wellspring of Life: they convey a powerful message that

1. you exist, you have a right to be visible and audible;
2. you have a right to be here, because;
3. you are good enough.

If you will do nothing else but A, pay attention and accept your own feelings you will see tremendous changes in yourself, as well as in your relationships.

Have you seen the movie Avatar? In it, the way these incarnations of deities greeted each other was "I see you", while putting a hand on their hearts, and bowing. *This* is what I am talking about. Wholeheartedly acknowledge the existence and such-ness of ... YOU!

Nature guides us into the next healthy action with the help of two types of strong sensations: comfort and discomfort, that represent love, and fear. This prompts us to reach for what we need, and recoil from what we don't. The body knows exactly *what* needs to happen, and the mind can figure out *how* to make that happen. But do not allow the mind to question the "what"! Do not allow the kids to rule the roost, or your dogs to bully you, because there is a fundamental hierarchy we all must respect, so that everyone is safe. The body is the master, and the mind is the butler, and that is just the way it is meant to be.

To offer no resistance to Life is to be in a
state of grace, ease and lightness.
Eckhart Tolle

If you have trouble paying attention to or accepting your Self please practice the above exercises, until you get better, so you can move on to the next step to self-parenting with love. You will find even more exercises in the Appendix.

My Dear Reader, look around and appreciate Nature's wisdom; the Sun comes up each morning, the leaves come back every year, so relax, you are in good hands. Massage yourself into trusting your body's intuition more and more; it will always guide you well!

Exercise 6: Accepting Self-Talk

1. Sit quietly, lingering with the most intense sensation in your body
2. Choose two of the statements below (the ones you like) and
3. Repeat them to yourself, 10 times, quietly, or out loud (pick the ones you like, or make up your own):
    "I love and accept myself in every way"
    "I am a wonderful person"
    "I trust my feelings and intuitions at all times"
    "I trust my body: it is my best friend"
    "It is OK for me to feel intensely"
    "It is safe for me to feel"
    "I accept the way I feel – I know that it is my Truth"
    "I trust my feelings"
    "I have a right to have feelings"
    "I love and accept my body for the truths it conveys to me"
    "I give myself permission to feel and to thrive"

If you are having a hard time with this, you will find more exercises for Acceptance in the Appendix. If you are still finding it hard to pay attention to or to accept your feelings as your truth, please remember that an hour of therapy a week for a while can do wonders.

SECOND STEP: B: Breathe, Be present

GOAL: To be able to stay present with the way you feel (rather than shut it down or distract yourself from it) so that it can inform you of your needs.

Stay here, quivering with each breath like a drop of mercury.

Rumi

Self-parenting with **A-B-C-D** will keep your Inner Child (IC) in active communication with your adult Self, so you will be informed about the truth, and able to help yourself. Once you have become aware of the most intense sensation or stress in your body, you must be able to linger with it long enough for it to inform you. Would you slam the door if there was a messenger with *the* most important info / greatest gift for you? I didn't think so.

The second step is self-soothing, in some constructive way pf course, just so that you do not react to the intensity in your body, but stay, and linger long enough for it to "talk". Self-soothing is compassionate presence. It is the key, it makes the difference between a door that is open, and one that is shut. Or, while we are at it, it is a window of opportunity that enables you to do something different with the discomfort, to not react, but respond to it. And so, self-soothing is the gateway to health. Although it is true that all four steps are instrumental in establishing and maintaining health, the ability to calm oneself down is the crown jewel of them all, because it prevents reactivity, and thus opens the way to communication and healthy action. But beware: this is the very point where we fail ourselves most often.

Self-soothing requires calming the body, and quieting the mind in the midst of sensation.

Focusing your mind on the body sensation itself, anchor it into that intensity you feel in your body and do the following two exercises. These will help you to linger longer, so you may be informed.

Close your mouth,
Block off your senses,
Blunt your sharpness,
Untie your knots,
Soften your glare,
Settle your dust.
This is the primal identity.
Lao Tzu

Calming the body

Exercise 1: Slow breathing

1. Place your hand on the spot of highest sensation in your body (or, if the only signal you found was frantic thoughts, place your hand on your front);
2. Slowly, inhale to the count of six, right into that sensation;
3. Hold the breath there for one or two counts, letting it nourish and soothe that spot, and then
4. Release your breath slowly, to the count of seven;
5. Repeat this three more times, soothing the sensation. The goal is not to make it go away (first we want to know what it came to say, remember?), rather to be able to sit with it for a little while.

Exercise 2: Progressive muscle relaxation

Take just two minutes to relax each muscle group from the top of your head to your toes, so your body does not clamp down around the sensation. This will slow and cease the alarm bells, allowing for a quiet conversation with the discomfort, to open and receive the message that the sensation is trying to bring to you. Remember, intensity is our friend! Just because it is uncomfortable, it does not mean it is mean – quite au contraire. It is designed to inform you of what you must do to be well - so befriend it!

- ♥ Starting with the top of your head, go progressively down visualizing each part of your body relaxing, letting go, and softening.
- ♥ You may imagine each part of you melting as a warm wave washes over you, or any other image that relaxes and soothes your body progressively from head to toe: muscles, bones, nerve endings, all the way down to your cells.

Quieting the mind

Often, our own minds act as an outside source of information – not exactly something to trust with your health. The mind has no access to the here and now, because it does not sense. Elayne Savage put it most aptly: "Instead of your "inner censors", pay attention to your "inner sensors".

The mind reasons, but makes no sense – pun intended! It operates on information gained from other places, times and people. Go to it for solutions of problems, but not for answers to what is true for you - for it can only guess, and approximate the truth, at best. The mind is a tool, a sharp pair of shears always moving, even when there is no problem in sight to solve. Unless you teach it to stop it will cut you up. Teach it to shut up and listen to the body, and stop the noise and distraction from the true source of the most vital information there is: what do I do next to be well?

The mind talks, the body knows.
The Buddha

Exercise 1: Positive self-talk

This awesome technique was first described in the 1980's by Shad Helmstetter in his book "What to Say When You Talk to Your Self".

1. Pay attention to what your mind is saying in reaction to the discomfort. If you catch any negative chatter that invalidates the truth of the sensation (e.g. "I am not feeling that", "I should not feel that", "I have no time for that", etc.), or tries to brush it off, by interpreting it - *as if* you already knew what it all means ("Oh, it's just because I shoveled snow")

STOP!

2. In order for the sensation to talk you must let it do so by switching off your mind's negativity.
3. Now, *shatter* that line it was saying, actually see it disintegrate. You do not want to negotiate with terrorists. The answer is no, I am not talking to you! I am talking to my body!
4. And now, *reverse* that negative message into its exact and clean opposite, one that has only positive words in it (the word "no" does not belong here!). For example, "I have a right to feel" "I trust my body's sensations", or "I love myself even when I am hurt" – an

antidote message that will effectively erase the original message and replace it with one that is positive and allowing.

5. And now, repeat this positive message to yourself, silently in your head, or out loud 30 times. This is what it takes to clean up the mess of negative self-talk. Think of it as if it were broken glass on your kitchen floor: you would sweep it about that many times to really make sure there is none left for someone to step into it.

He started to sing, as he tackled the thing
That could not be done, and he did it.
Edgar Albert Guest

Do this every time you notice your mind shooting off negative messages, so you cultivate a stance of humility and acceptance toward your body's profound intelligence. As you do this repeatedly, day in, and day out, you will find that your mind will tire of its shenanigans, and get in line with the program, becoming progressively more and more a supporter on its own accord. Remember, self-discipline is one of the two main components of healthy self-parenting, along with self-love. Use it to control your mind! We must exercise self-discipline consistently when it comes to negative self-talk: it is *always* destructive, do not believe or put up with it for a minute! And be diligent with this exercise until you become *allergic* to negative messages. They are pathogenic!

STOP!

SHATTER!

REVERSE!

REPEAT!

Exercise 2: Positive imagery

As you sit with the intense sensation in your body, you can calm yourself also by imagining sitting in a safe place, where you may have been before.

1. Think of a time and place when you felt the best, the most relaxed and safe, where you could be completely yourself.
2. <u>Look</u> around in that place... <u>smell</u> the fragrances in the air...<u>hear</u> the sounds...<u>feel</u> the sensations on your skin...notice if there is a particular <u>taste</u> in your mouth connected with this experience...and above all, <u>sense</u> the safety, the peace, the serenity on a visceral level.

As you recall this memory (real or imagined!) you are triggering/creating the body memory of it, and you are flooded with joyful, peaceful, relaxed hormones; your muscles relax more, and you are surrounding the original uncomfortable sensation with peace and acceptance. This is not to extinguish it (although it will lower the intensity of the sensation), no, it must talk to you first! This is just to be able to sit with it and listen, like a doctor would sit with a patient in pain, with an open mind and heart. *Now* you are on the right track to listen inward, to your Inner Child.

> *Terry was of course very upset when some people treated her badly at her wedding. In her anger she thought over and over how mean some people are – and she was right. However, in the process she forgot to soothe herself, to make herself feel better by letting it go. When we feel hurt, all too often we forget to run to our inner selves' rescue, and instead, we get stuck focusing on others in judgment and blame. In self-parenting terms this would spell abandonment, right in the middle of the need.*

You will find more exercises for **B**, or self-soothing in the Appendix. Do take the time to practice your self-soothing skills, they truly are worth every ounce of effort, because the bulk of what we truly need in life is soothing. These skills will pay you back in spades. As a bonus, the more you practice, the sooner they will come to you automatically when you need them most – and *this is the goal.*

Exercise 3: Rampages of Appreciation

Gratitude unlocks the fullness of life. It turns what we have into enough, and more. It turns denial into acceptance, chaos to order, confusion to clarity. It can turn a meal into a feast, a house into a home, a stranger into a friend. Gratitude makes sense of our past, brings peace for today, and creates a vision for tomorrow.

Melody Beattie

This term I borrowed from Esther Hicks offers a graphic impression of the practice of enthusiastically affirming all that is good in your life. Make it a habit, and you will feel marvelous! The simple act of verbalizing the positives makes them more real, carves them into your awareness, and prompts you to notice more of them, and more often. Again, *each thought is a self-fulfilling prophecy, meaning appreciation will also bring forth more of its kind both within you and in your world.*

I. List to yourself, silently, or out loud, all the things you are grateful for, about you, your life, your family, your job, and everything else you can think of.

2. Do this once a day for ever, and ever, and ever... the more you do it, the easier it will flow, and become a "rampage" on its own impetus.

Exercise 4: Affirmations

Affirmations are powerful self-soothers. They are positive, short statements in the present tense. They are a form of self-hypnosis, and as such they are extremely powerful tools to heal your relationship to yourself. The messages we receive (whether from ourselves or others) when repeated over time solidify in our consciousness as beliefs, which, with more repetition go on to create feelings, the very things we base our behaviors and choices on. You can reach into your own belief system and tweak it to better suit your health by using affirmations.

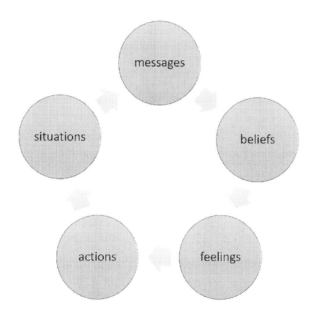

Messages are the building blocks and the foundation of our whole existence. Words, attitudes, behaviors, and even food and our environment is made of information, of a certain energetic vibration that ultimately constitutes our very being. Repeated messages over time solidify as beliefs, that in turn form feelings, that lead to actions that create our life's situations; these then go on to corroborate the original messages. We create our lives through messages, and this is why it is instrumental to feed ourselves a hefty daily dose of positive ones; they have a knack for fulfilling themselves (see above)!

Often people get stumped by the fact that they don't believe what the affirmation says. That is not only okay, it is to be expected. In fact, the very reason you must use affirmations is because you do not believe them – not yet, anyway. You will, however believe them down the road, the more you use them, the sooner. It is not lying to yourself, it is simply choosing what you want to believe. What you believe today is not because it is true, but because it was repeated to you by others, and then by yourself, over time with enough frequency for it to stick. This is a case of "fake it 'til you make it"!

Here, let me just make sure that we are on the same page about this: affirmations are not supposed to talk you out of feeling bad! They must be used *after* you have acknowledged and accepted your feelings of discomfort, as a way to heal yourself from the emotional effects of old, destructive messages (like for instance, "I am not good enough").

The best times to use affirmations are first thing upon awakening, and last thing before falling asleep; you are still or already in your bed, your body is relaxed and your brain's frequency is in "alpha" (the stage between alert and asleep). This is when the mind is most open and able to soak up new information without questioning it. Yeah, baby!

1. Choose two affirmations (see below) for one "session".
2. Take the first one, and repeat it to yourself 30-40 times (you can count on your fingers).
3. You can do this
   - mindlessly, like with the rosary, or
   - mindfully, imagining that you believe and feel the truth, the energy of the statement in your body, with each repetition.

It is a good idea to repeat affirmations to yourself throughout the day as well, every time you are doing something automatic, like driving a car, cleaning the house, etc. Switch off the radio and repeat, repeat, because the more you do it, the sooner you will feel better. *The trick is to stay with it,* however: don't stop when you start feeling better, because it takes a long-long time (years) to change old beliefs! Remember: repetition is the mother of all knowledge! You are best off setting your mind to using affirmations like you brush or floss your teeth: each day, for the rest of your life, to clean away debris, and plaque. It is mental flossing!

Here are some of my personal favorites:
"Every day, in every way my life is getting better and better" (coined by Émile Coué, the father of hypnosis)
"I always do the best I can with what I have"
"I just do my best and let go of the outcome"
"I let the chips fall where they may"
"I love and accept myself in every way"
"I trust my feelings completely"
"I am a good person: I love and appreciate myself just the way I am"

You can make up your own affirmations, like this:

1. How would you like to feel? Write those feelings down (e.g. good enough, peaceful, energized, etc.)
2. Take one feeling, and mold it into a brief statement that is:
    - Positive (ONLY positive words are allowed! The word "not" is not positive!)
    - In the present tense, as if it was already true
    - Powerful (meaning it really strikes a chord with you!)
3. Have your affirmations handy, by your bed, taped on your bathroom mirror, and in your handbag, so you can use them throughout the day.
4. Choose two affirmations for each "sitting". Repeat one affirmation 30 times, and then the other.

Negative Thinking: the Stress Generator

There is nothing either good or bad but thinking makes it so.

Shakespeare, Hamlet

If you look around your immediate surroundings right now, I bet there is not much not to like or accept just the way it is. Mind you, the moment you say to yourself something negative about anything, you just rejected it. That instantaneously puts you at odds with your world, creating an inner – and possibly outer - battle. When you indiscriminately give negative labels to things in your life you are liable to be caught up in that, and label yourself as well. In fact, this attitude may be a reflection of you rejecting your own feelings in the first place. That is when the enemy is within the doors, and you wake up and go to sleep with the clatter of swords in your ears – IF it lets you sleep, that is!

When you let yourself be judgmental under stress, negativity in thoughts and actions is a hurtful act to the already hurting Self. We are learning machines, and we believe every bit of information we are fed, even if the source is our own Selves. So be careful with what you say to yourself, because you will believe it, and then feel it, and then act accordingly, thus kicking in the next, downward spiraling cycle of the same.

Negative words spell stress. Every word is a self-fulfilling prophecy, every act a vortex: they produce more of their kind. What we say to ourselves, or to others is either a blessing or a curse: it will either spiral us up, or down. What we do is a blueprint, a precedent with a magnet on it, pulling similar actions into its track. This is why negativity is the single greatest pathogen on Earth. It begets more of itself. It will disintegrate anything of value.

Think of it this way: painful experiences, stresses are not negativity, but normal parts of life. THEY are the germs, and bacteria that are always there, present everywhere, doing excellent work at keeping life in balance. They are not the ones responsible for illness. Do not look for something to blame "out there"; it is what it is. In reality, what makes us ill is usually not something external (unless it is extreme, like serious pollution, or abuse) but the lack of enough immunity – i.e. positive thoughts and experiences – present in the face of these givens.

"The mind is its own place, and in itself
Can make a heav'n of hell, a hell of heav'n".
Milton, Paradise Lost

When you are hurting in any way, physically or emotionally, what your balance hinges on is your physical or emotional immune system's capacity to overcome it. Your experience of love, acceptance, care, and soothing buried in your subconscious memory is what constitutes your emotional immune system. So when you are hurting, or injured in any way, make sure you tap into that reservoir of positive messages and experiences: they are your medicine chest. When you encounter your pain with loving, accepting, caring and soothing thoughts and actions by your own Self, you will also be more likely to ask for it from others. Conversely, if you ignore your pain, or if you blame (or frighten, or shame, or attack) yourself for it, you are effectively freezing your emotional immune system with negativity, thus preventing it from doing its work. This will unavoidably lead to more pain, add insult on top of injury. Attacking or ignoring an ailing system translates into rubbing the injury further in – what an insult! This is how downward spirals begin, resulting in physical and/or emotional illness. When there is no barrier to the normally occurring physical or emotional pain the invader pervades, goes "viral" inside of you.

This is what is called "suffering" in the Buddhist tradition. Suffering is entirely avoidable – stress and pain are not. The Buddhist style of self-care and self-parenting involves primarily meditation. Sitting with one's own feelings is exquisitely healing. Staying present (i.e. responsive by practicing **A** and **B**) with your feelings is vital to self- love. This is the gently internal Eastern style of self-care.

To complete the circle of loving yourself, it is necessary to communicate (**C**) with your Self, and then with others, and then do (**D**) what you find out is necessary for feeling better. These are the last two steps of self-love - coming right up!

Everything is based on mind, is led by mind, and is fashioned by mind.
If you speak and act with a polluted mind, suffering will follow you,
as the wheels of the oxcart follow the footsteps of the ox...
If you speak and act with a pure mind, happiness will follow you,
as a shadow clings to a form.
The Buddha

My Kind Reader, commit to being positive to yourself. Be the one who holds you! Be the first one who loves and accepts you just the way you are; it is what's right, and healthy and you deserve it. Practice this, and it will come easier and easier.

The Organ of Negativity – The Unchecked Mind

Better to have two hundred enemies on the outside
than one on the inside.
Chinese proverb

The single most destructive instrument of self-abuse and self-neglect is the Mind. If you let it bully you, you will be scared, worried, anxious, angry, and in general riled up. If you let it filter out the negatives from a sea of positives you will be miserable. Not kosher. What you need is soothing in the midst of the storm we call life. The mind has the power to generate a tsunami inside of you, or it can be taught to smooth out any ruffled edges.

Given that the mind is the central tower of control, our whole health depends on what it does in the moment of uncomfortable sensation. Does it kiss the discomfort with approval and curiosity like it should? Or does it invalidate, question or negate the truth? Or accelerate into frantic thinking? Very often, yes. This is an age-old mechanism, that we learned sometime early in our history to try to think our way out of life threatening situations. At this point in our evolution, however, we are using the mind to think our way out of feeling bad – a very dangerous proposition, given that feeling bad is our main survival mechanism. Not to mention that it does not work: we cannot will our feelings away just as we cannot wish the weather to stop.

The unchecked mind is a magnet for misery. One way to describe this is that negativity, the default mode of the unchecked mind, is abuse and neglect: you are abusing yourself with the negative self-talk, and thereby neglecting to give yourself what you really need. You might remember: abuse and neglect lead to disconnect, an attitude of absence from the current experience, from the present moment. Why should I stay present *for this* - and click, you disconnect. Is your Inner Parent a deadbeat? Disconnect is the mother of all ills, because, again, the positive parent is absent, and thus there is no one to take care of me, the hurting Self. In the absence of the Inner Parent there is no positive self-care... and that is when things spiral down emotionally, physically and spiritually.

With the militia of love and compassion
Subdue your own mind.
Togmay Sangpo

Have you noticed that you can only convince yourself for so long that you are not, or should not feel what you are feeling? And then, reality sets in, often with a vengeance - and now you feel even worse. This is because what you are feeling is the truth – *even if you disagree!* All the rationalizations, distractions, numbing, frantic pace of thought or action will simply not dissolve the way we feel, they just distract from the experience. Instead of helping, thinking will suspend your self-care in the midst of the discomfort, which, unattended, grows and deepens in order to grab your attention.

Thoughts are like frightened children: they will throw fearful or mean messages at you. For instance, you may have a headache, and call yourself an idiot, because you did not go to bed early enough the night before. Blame on top of hurt. Or, you may have an important interview the next day, and your mind might say discouraging things like "Who am I to get that job, anyway? There are so many smarter people than me". Be careful, do remember how very suggestible (and gullible) we all are, and do not feed yourself junk, lest you want to believe it. This is how the shenanigans of the mind bind us into a knot right when we need help the most.

Stop thinking, and end your problems.

Lao Tzu

Another mistake of the Mind is to ignore the sensation. Too much thinking is overreacting, or aggressing. Too little, that is lack of attention and awareness, is neglecting, or being passive when our deliberate focus is called upon. This stance is also likely to escalate the sensation into pain, or even a condition, again, because there is no one tending the shop! Nature will not let us die of hunger if we ignore it, it will simply escalate it, until it is so unbearable that there is no denying it.

Have mercy on your soul, stop the insanity, that machinery of the mind that will not let you just be, just feel, and just be present with the sensation without having to become an evil step-monster to it. We think too much as it is. *Train* yourself to allow yourself to just feel good, or bad, to linger with whatever sensation you feel in your body – and it will become easier with practice. Be present for the experience of the moment, feel that "delicious ache", see it, taste it, soak it up. Linger longer. Love it and live it. *Notice, trust your body and be informed, so you may help yourself. This is what I call foolproof design, Made in Nature.*

When the body's intelligence declines,
Cleverness and knowledge step forth.

Lao Tzu

In ancient Chinese thought the mind was called "crazy monkeys" or "wild horses". It is like a sharp pair of scissors that will cut even when there is nothing to resolve. Since Life is not a problem to be resolved, do not use your mind as your main guide. Instead, watch it, or it will cut you up and make you bleed into misery. Would you ask your scissors about what you should do? No, you would probably find out what you should do first, and then see if your scissors would be a helpful tool to achieve that goal.

Such is the mind exactly. When it has no "assignment", it starts running around destroying things. By default, it turns negative, because it is impressionable, and does not have the perspective of the whole. (On this subject check out Jill Bolte Taylor's talk on TED.com. Incredible!) In lack of structure, order, and a strong and loving parent figure the world is a scary place - and the mind becomes frantic and negative. The mind must be appreciated for what it is, a tool, and disciplined, for what it is not: the boss. Eckhart Tolle did a stellar job exploring the pain the untamed mind causes in his classic book, The Power of Now.

Here is a list of the mind's typical ways of becoming frantic and unruly. I recommend you establish a ZERO TOLERANCE policy for any of the following:

Negative self-talk	Examples
• bullying	I bet you can't ___, you are such a sissy
• blaming	it's all my fault
• shaming	I am nothing
• criticizing	Why can't you just lose weight?
• name calling	I am stupid (lazy, weak, ugly)
• catastrophizing	If I eat ice cream, my arteries will clog and I will die

- worrying   What if _____?

- despairing   There is no point, this is the end

- threatening   If I don't listen to them, they will hate me

- generalizing   This *always* happens to me. Life sucks. I
                                    never catch a break"

- polarized thinking (all   If I can't do ___ perfectly
  or nothing, black or   I can't do it at all
  white, perfectionism)

- fear-mongering   They will laugh at me, and make fun of me;
                                    They will think I am stupid; I will throw
                                    up, and everybody will see it

- hate-mongering   Women/men are all jerks; (fill in a minority) are
                                    all out to get our jobs/lands/money

- labeling (negatively)   I am a failure (weak, not good enough)

- judging   I am lazy (stupid, selfish); Stop whining

- demeaning   I am not good at anything

- minimizing (what is   It does not matter, some other time...
  important to you)

- ignoring   I have better / more important things to do

- distracting (from what   Feeling sad? Go shopping (working,
  matters to you)   bungee jumping, etc.)

- interpreting   I am just tired...

- should-ing   I should _____
                                    I shouldn't _____

- sarcasm   Yeah, right, like you should be the one
                                    they choose

If a problem is fixable, if a situation is such that you
can do something about it, then there is no need to worry.
If it's not fixable, then there is no help in worrying.
There is no benefit in worrying whatsoever.
Dalai Lama XIV.

As you eliminate these from your self-talk you will lose any proneness to talk to others like this as well. A good way to gage whether or not what you are saying to yourself is OK is to ask yourself: would I say this to someone I love when she is hurting? If not, how is it fair to talk to yourself like this? Time to

STOP

        SHATTER

                REVERSE

                        REPEAT.

What negative self-talk does is adding insult to injury. You were stressed in the first place... now you are feeling even worse. To make matters worse, your relationships will suffer, because you will allow the people around you talk to you like this (remember the blind-spot argument?) and then resent them for it. Also, even though you may not say these things to others, you are thinking it about yourself, so by default, and by extension they *are* your thoughts about other people, situations, things, circumstances, and Life in general. Your own personal well must be clean – make sure you don't inadvertently poison it!

Okay, maybe your mind probably does most of the above, on a good day (or could YOU be the one exception?); case in point, do not worry! These are just habits, very bad ones, but nonetheless habits, and habits can be changed! It is only learning, that needs to be unlearned and re-learned - and it is never too late for that, trust me on this. Again, we are learning machines, and this is not even hard. It does, however, take focus, self-discipline and practice. On the long haul, as you practice good mental hygiene habits, they, in turn will become your automatic pilot, your second nature, more and more so. GOOD! With every bit of practice you are building a new trend, a new second nature that will automatically spring forth in any given any situation.

If you are a true worrier try the Worry Antidote exercise in the Appendix.

Two Wolves – A Cherokee Parable

"An old Cherokee chief was teaching his grandson about life...
'A fight is going on inside me,' he said to the boy.
'It is a terrible fight and it is between two wolves.
One is evil – he is anger, envy, sorrow, regret, greed,
arrogance, self-pity, guilt, resentment, inferiority, lies,
false pride, superiority, self-doubt, and ego.
The other is good – he is joy, peace, love, hope,
serenity, humility, kindness, benevolence, empathy,
generosity, truth, compassion, and faith.
This same fight is going on inside you
and inside every other person, too.'
The grandson thought about it for a minute
and then asked his grandfather,
'Which wolf will win?'
The old chief simply replied,
'The one you feed.'"

Now, the thing with these negative mental habits is that they are like an auto-immune disease: they were designed in the first place to protect you by categorizing things so you can handle them, or by expecting the worst, so nothing or no one can shock you. In lack of enough love and safety we learn early in life to protect ourselves from the pain with our thoughts. However, once the original situation is gone and we grow up, frantic thinking loses its function. It turns on you, the thinker of these thoughts, and starts to attack you, strapping you of joy, and peace. This is a matter of utmost importance, so no, my dear, you do not get to sit on your laurels and just forget about it! If you have negative thought patterns it is imperative that you change them; without positive thinking there is no mental, emotional, or even physical health. In fact, health and happiness go hand in hand, because feeling good is a symptom of your body being well. It is all one system!

Don't tell me that worry doesn't do any good.
I know better. The things I worry about don't happen!
Unknown

If you practice any type of negative self-talk it is as if you were popping depressant pills. (If you are taking antidepressants this might be the reason why they don't work!) The way to kick the habit is to practice Positive Self-Talk, the way I described it earlier (with affirmations and the four-step thought reversal). You will need to build in a Mind Monitor first, so that you will notice when it is happening, and quickly replace it, in real time, with the positive opposite. Repeating positive messages to yourself a million times a day is the very mechanism that produced those negative thoughts and beliefs in the first place – first by others, and then by your own self.

To sum it up, these are the skills that will help you soothe yourself:

1. slow breathing
2. progressive relaxation of your body
3. positive self-talk
4. positive imagery
5. monitoring your mind, like this:

Exercise 3. Building in a Mind Monitor

1. First thing in the morning, upon awakening, set your intention on monitoring your mind throughout the day for any negative messages to yourself. Do this by emphatically *saying* to yourself:

2. *"Today, I am going to notice any negative thoughts in my head and correct them"*

3. Consider your Mind Monitor an officer of Homeland Security, who will simply not allow any terrorists into your space. *Imagine* this highly trained and reliable agent patrolling your mind through the day, as it comments on you and others, and *pulling all the stops* the moment it notices any shade of negativity: blame, criticism, labels, sarcasm, rejection, pessimism, etc.

4. You Mind Monitor is trained to never negotiate with the enemy, never concede to any part of its message. No negativity is allowed, to any degree! Every time you catch one, use your Positive Self-Talk skills: stop, shatter, reverse, and repeat the exact, clean opposite 30 times.

If you have trouble quieting your mind, you will find more exercises in the Appendix. If you are still finding it hard to soothe yourself, your mind and body, please remember how much good you a little therapy would do.

My Worthy Reader, DO NOT THINK or ACT UNDER THE INFLUENCE of stress, just FEEL! Soothe yourself, soothe yourself, and soothe yourself some more.

THIRD STEP: C: Communication

Goal: To let your body's sensations inform you about your specific feelings and needs.

1. Communication with Your Self

Let the body's doings speak openly now,

Without your saying a word,

As a student's walking behind a teacher

Says, "This one knows more clearly

Then I the way".

Rumi

You now have paid **A**ttention to your body's sensations. You have **B**reathed into them, and soothed yourself with them to be able to stay tuned in. Take a piece of paper, or use the Authenticity Process Sheet (in Part Five, Exercise 5.) to plug in the information you receive as you go about your feelings and needs, each in the appropriate column. It is better to write it all down because usually a lot of information will come forth, and often rapidly.

In psychological circles there is a handy little acronym for feelings, H.A.L.T. It stands for:

1. hungry
2. angry
3. lonely, and
4. tired.

These are the core feelings of discomfort that must be communicated to yourself and then, to others. These are the ones that get us into trouble unless shared. Of course, we also have feelings of comfort (see the last column of the chart below), and it is best to communicate them, too, because when shared, they build an "emotional immune system" for the relationship: if it receives consistent deposits of good vibes that were verbalized, it will withstand more stress! Before you start the next exercise, glance through this Feelings Chart. This will activate your vocabulary of words for feelings.

Feelings' Chart

HUNGRY*	ANGRY	LONELY	TIRED	COMFORTABLE
Wanting	Frustrated	Numb	Exhausted	Powerful
Needing	Irritable	Abandoned	Depleted	Fulfilled
Craving	Betrayed	Empty	Sick	Energized
Missing	Abused	Disconnected	Powerless	Grateful
D Desperate for	Sad	Confused	Defeated	Healthy
Expecting	Guilty	Vulnerable	Sleepy	Connected
Eager	Blamed	Afraid	D Discouraged	Relaxed
Jealous	Judged	Anxious	Weary	Peaceful
Envious	Criticized	Distant	Weak	Trusting
T Thirsty (for)	D Disappointed	Insecure	Fatigued	Secure

*According to the Ayurveda we have a hundred "hungers". The things we may feel hungry for on any given day include love, attention, acceptance, energy, kindness, approval, food, drink, time, money, clarification, conversation, information, movement, air, comfort, companionship, fun, order, purpose, direction, peace, harmony, relaxation, rest, sleep, care, touch, sex, freedom, closeness, independence, space, forgiveness, etc.

Exercise 1. Eliciting Feelings

1. Have your Authenticity Process Sheet and a pen ready.

2. Next, take another deep breath into the spot of highest sensation. Hook your attention into that area, let it fascinate over that sensation. Switch off your thoughts once again, making sure they don't "bark". This is NOT a thinking exercise – it is more like wake-dreaming, calling forth your intuition.

3. As you focus on the sensation, and nothing else, ask that sensation the question: "How am I feeling? What are the feelings you are expressing?" and

4. Let any *words or images*, or even *physical urges* come to you. Pay attention, with a subtle perception, because the information will not come with a bang, it will arrive on butterfly wings. Any distraction, internal or external will make it startle and instantly leave. Your focus on the spot of sensation is essential in picking up on this dream-like information.

5. Write down – under Feelings - any words that come to you, with no judgment, even if it doesn't make any sense. This is the truth, know it or not, like it or not. Believe it.

   If what comes to you is an image, ask yourself "how do I feel when I see this image?" Again, as words come to you, write them down.

6. Ask four more times, slowly, the same question, and write the answers down. You now will have at least three feeling words written on your page.

Continue to silence your mind throughout this exercise – and no judgment, no questions, no doubt, no interpretation! Anchor your attention onto the spot of sensation by visualizing it, and breathing into it, or even by placing your hand over it. That is the place you are talking to.

Exercise 2. Eliciting Needs

1. Staying focused on the body sensation take another deep breath into it.

2. Ask the sensation: "What do I need *from myself* to feel better? What do I need to do, or say, or be like to feel better?"

3. Notice any subtle information; it can be an image, a word, a thought, a color, smell, taste, or even an urge. Allow any and all information to bubble up straight from the sensation.

4. Write down anything that comes to you under Needs – even if you disagree, or don't know how you could ever do this. Let this process guide you; let go of controlling it.

5. Refocus on the sensation and ask it
    - What will it look like when I do this?   – write down the answer
    - How do I do this?   – write down the answer
    - When?   – write down the answer
    - How often?   – write down the answer
    - How much?   – write down the answer
    - With what?   – write down the answer
    - With whom?   – write down the answer

    All the answers from your body go under the column "WWWHHH".

6. Continue asking for specifics until you have an actual set of actions that can be plugged into your calendar, with day, time, duration, frequency, etc. DO NOT ASK YOUR MIND! ASK YOUR BODY ONLY! If your mind start budding in, take a deep breath, and refocus it on the sensation in your body (much like you would if someone barged in onto a conversation you are having with someone else.)

7. Refocus, caress that sensation of yours with your breath, thanking it for the truths it is bringing to you.

8. Ask the question "What else do I need to do, or say, or be like to feel better?"

9. Repeat steps 3 through 7 and write down what you find out. Do this three more times, to exhaust all possible information your body is storing.
10. Continue asking about other needs, until you are not getting any more answers.
11. In the last round ask more specifically "What do I need to do in my relationship to myself to feel better?" – write down the answers, with all the WWWHHH specifics.
12. Take out your phone, or calendar and plug the action steps you received into it. Feel free to set alarms for them, to make sure that you will have the time and the reminders to carry these actions out. They are the ones that will bring about actual changes in your life. These are the very steps of self-help – everything before them is just leading up to being able to help yourself feel better in a wholesome and organic way.

Without actually asking your inner Self about your feelings and needs – without communicating with yourself, that is – you can only help yourself haphazardly, guessing, but not knowing *exactly* what will hit the spot. It is much like going shopping blindfolded. You will get something, but most probably not exactly what you needed. Only the body knows what is immediate and present; the mind can only tap into other times, places, or other people's experiences.

Notice that in this step there is no exploring the reasons why you feel the way you do. Reasons are a function of the intellect; looking for them would be a fatal distraction from this subtle process of tapping into your intuition. If you notice getting distracted from your body by thinking about *why* you feel this way, and what you can do about it, STOP!!! Breathe, re-focus on the sensation, and repeat the two questions, one by one, several times each. Your only job is to take notes, like a good secretary. Do not question anything, just go with it – and you will learn that "it" – your body, your intuition, Nature – always guides you right.

Constant Communication: Tethering Your Inner Child

To heal means to meet ourselves in a new way –
in the newness of each moment ...
The vastness of our being meeting each moment
wholeheartedly whether it holds pleasure or pain.
Then the healing goes deeper than we ever imagined,
deeper than we ever dreamed.

Stephen Levine

We are still talking about self-parenting with love and limits. Of course parenting never stops: you are always there, available and attentive to your children. Similarly, there needs to be a constant checking in with our Inner Child. To the very least you can ask yourself four questions throughout the day, summed up in the well-known acronym HALT: Hungry? Angry? Lonely? Tired? If so, what is the sensation associated with that feeling saying about what you need, when, and how? And then, just do it!

Better yet, why not scan your body as you go, and notice any squeaking, any discomfort that means "the baby is crying"? Tethering yourself means paying attention to how you feel each moment, and gage your next step accordingly, even if this means you have to cancel a plan, or possibly disappoint someone. You would not let your child out of your sight in a department store, would you? Do not let your Inner Child out of your sight, because when you do, you will lose connection with yourself, which leads to loneliness, frustration, anxiety, or even illness. Then, others around you will unavoidably have to pay the price.

You know your Inner Child is calling upon you for help when you have a body sensation. This child is completely truthful, candid and pure, and wants nothing more than to trust you, the Inner Parent, with his feelings.

If you did not check in with yourself constantly, you would be dragging your Inner Child through the day without even a peek at how she is doing. Flying through the mall, zipping through chores and duties with a cranky child in tow. What would that mean in parenting terms? Both abuse *and* neglect.

Over time, if we continue to ignore our feelings they literally "burn out", hence the emptiness and despondency of depression. The Inner Child that carries our feelings was left alone and got disconnected, lost. Of course, you and I would NEVER leave and actual child alone in a store, but then again, we are usually nicer to our kids than to our own Selves. This is exactly the point: to become the kindest, sweetest, most attentive parent to our own selves; to bring the skills home to ourselves, so that we may finally feel connected, and have peace within the ranks. The Inner Child must receive what you would give your beloved Outer Child, and be promoted to the rank of your First Born - which is what he truly is! Indeed, without positive attention to the inner, child-Self we feel disconnected, lost, lonely, frustrated, and ultimately depressed.

Health, authenticity, or inner peace requires slowing down, the very prerequisite for excellent communication and collaboration between these two parts. In this internal tethering the Inner Parent is connected with an invisible string to the Inner Child, constantly asking "how are you feeling now... and now...and now?", taking the child's answers as the truth, and acting accordingly, - as long as the parent deems it healthy and necessary. "Are you hungry? Angry? Lonely? Tired?" (H-A-L-T). These are the questions posed to the Inner Child each hour of each day, and the answers honored. Of course, if what you crave is not healthy and/or necessary, then the Inner Parent needs to set a limit, and give you positive discipline.

This type of relationship to our Selves brings a true sense of safety and security into our psyches, because we will always feel connected and taken care of. This is the foundation from which we can find the same connection, care, and safety in the outside world.

So, do not ladle life into yourself, do not crowd and complicate your life with too many things, people or activities. This would be focusing externally for what you need, only to leave you feeling disconnected, dissatisfied, empty, as well as overwhelmed. The measure of how much of anything is the right amount, and when is the right time for it is not what Aunt Beth is saying, but how you feel in your body this very moment. If it relaxes at the thought or sight of the next thing/person/activity, well then, bring it on! If, on the other hand it constricts and tenses up, do set a limit to your own urge, by saying "no, dear, you may not... (go to, do, or have) that", whatever it is that you were fancying. The way to tether your inner, true Self is by savoring each and every moment with a baby spoon. There is always more, if it feels good. Simply, one step at a time you will stay present with your experience and thus live fully.

When the Inner Child and the Inner Parent get along, then actions and choices are aligned with our feelings. In this parent-child relationship the Parent is all grown-up, mature, knows the rules, has good judgment, skills, can articulate thoughts and feelings, and has all the resources necessary to keep him- or herself safe and well. In fact, this part of us is already doing all that out in the world, usually helping others that we love. The Child part of us feels, is joyous or sad, screams for help, or food, or protection, or guidance, in other words, the part that has no qualms about needing and asking for what it needs, and simply does not know how to lie - so it does not. Give it what it needs and all is well. *This is the primal relationship, the fundamental attachment.*

Attachment

Allow me a short diversion here into what this issue is known as in the field of psychology: attachment. When a baby is born, it learns to feel safe by getting what it needs, there and then. This forms a trusting bond, or attachment to the primary care-giver. A healthy attachment is at the very foundation of a healthy life, because through it we learn to *trust*, by gaining the experience of being connected, responded to, and important.

There are only two kinds of attachment: secure or insecure. Early care fosters a sense of security in childhood as well as for later relationships. Early abuse or neglect fosters insecurity. Abuse leads to what researchers call anxious, or disorganized attachment, while neglect creates ambivalent/resistant, or avoidant attachment (Ainsworth, M. 1967, Main, M.1986).

Trust is our only solace, it tells us we are not alone – the ultimate threat to a human, the ultimate collective being. We all need someone to lean on, for security. For a baby that fundamental connection must be a loving care-taker.

As adults, we have two choices for a fundamental connection like that: external or internal. If you do not forge a primary focus on your own feelings, you are abandoning yourself. Thus, by default, you will expect happiness to come from external things, like objects, or situations, or conditions, or money, power, position, youth, or even other people. In lack of a solid "inner attachment" you are bound to be let down, because things and relationships change – and your hope for security and safety is right out the window!

Patterns of thinking also qualify as external "tethers": premade judgments, opinions, "should's" and "should not's": if you rely on them for what is good and helpful will often put you at a war with yourself, and others. Not good for creating health and balance, right? Tethering yourself to externals will stifle your growth and hurt your health. It is like hanging on to the shore of the river, rather than letting it take you safely to harbor. Because it will, every time! Try it, if you don't believe it.

Resc-you

Paradoxically, the only stable point of reference in life is the "river" of our feelings. This is the one and only cornerstone for a fundamental connection: the ever fluctuating, fluid flow of our feelings. I cannot emphasize enough that feelings are Nature's way of keeping us alive and well. The intelligence of Mother Nature, God, or the Universe is expressed in the humble, ever-changing physical sensations we feel in our bodies each moment. Tether yourself to your feelings, and you will be gently floating in the river of life, with trust and faith.

Imagine taking your little child self by the hand and walking through life together in peace, harmony and mutual understanding. Focusing internally FIRST is the way health, peace and balance are achieved. You do this, and you are doing the best you can in this world. If you skip this and try to achieve health, peace and balance in places external to you (like in someone else's life), it will crumble, because the foundation is missing. Nothing survives on good intentions. We must organically build it from the ground up. Then, what you have on the inside, the qualities and patterns you are cultivating in your relationship with yourself will effortlessly flow into the things outside of you.

Commit to tethering your inner Self, by asking continually how you feel, and what you need. Kind, warm, non-judgmental of how you really are at this very moment you connect within. This is the primordial experience of safety in intimacy.

2. Communication with Others: Assertiveness

Be who you are and say what you feel
Because those who mind don't matter,
And those who matter don't mind.
Dr. Seuss

Assertiveness is clear communication, language used at its crispest to ask for (or say yes to) what you need, and to set limits (or say no) to what hurts you. Without it we would not get the majority of our needs met, and we would not be safe. Assertiveness is a learned skill that is as precise as it is useful in creating a good life.

Without language used effectively there is no survival, let alone thriving. Did you know that language is the very reason we are stumping on this Earth? We are the descendants of the Cro-Magnons, who pushed the much more primitive Neanderthals into extinction because they had the benefit of language to ensure effective collaboration. Language is the main tool of cooperation among humans, which in turn is the very reason for our survival as a species.

God created the child, that is, your wanting,
So that it might cry out, so that milk might come.
Cry out! Don't be stolid and silent
With your pain. Lament! And let the milk
Of loving flow into you.
Rumi

The ability to speak is our fifth limb, what we use to reach for the things we need that we cannot walk to or grab with our hands. Basic necessities, like appreciation, understanding, clarification, acceptance, or safety, just to name a few. These are things we may ache for in a given situation, and only get if we ask - and then mean it. Assertiveness is language used precisely, positively, and in real time; it's the foremost skill in establishing and maintaining health, the crown jewel of self-help, a glorious flower that can only grow in a well-maintained soil made of body awareness (A), self-soothing (B), and communication with one's Self (C).

Many of my needs can only be fulfilled if I ask, if I assert myself. When I do get what I need, I flourish, I am happy, relaxed and peaceful, and people around me are the better for it. When I do not get what I need, I get cranky, angry, and ill. The more my need-fulfillment is frustrated, the more need I have, and this downward spiral leads to bigger problems, including emotional, physical or relational illness. It is just the way it works. And the magic wand is assertiveness.

I have met many people who have a hard time speaking their truth. Do you feel guilty for asking for what you need? I hear this all the time: I don't want to burden anyone, I don't want to be selfish, or high maintenance. You *are* high maintenance, my dear, like it or not – we all are! By nature we are complex beings with a multitude of ever changing needs, so yes, maintenance is just what the doctor ordered.

Many girls - and even boys - are raised to be complacent and compliant, to be seen and not heard; this sets you up for feeling guilty when you have something to say or when you need something. A prime case for when the old law must be broken and rewritten, because *talking is good and necessary for the health and well-being of everyone involved.*

Speaking your truth is more often than not part of **D**, doing what it takes to be well and get your needs met. So be real and authentic by actually speaking up, and then mind your tone, pace, volume, verbiage, and body language. Do not escalate in any way, so that you may be heard exactly the way you mean it.

"No!": Your Best Friend

For optimal self-care you may need to amp up your ability to say "no" – a healthy person's best friend! Saying no to others is the cornerstone of emotional health. Imagine you are a gardener: saying no is equal to putting a fence around your garden in a deer infested area. The world is infested with people will feast on your energy that is your garden. Not because they are bad, but because they *are*, and this is nature's way. If they knew that this is hurting you, they would stop (most of them, anyway).

—❧—

"Enough" is a word for the Wise.
African Proverb

—❧—

Saying no protects what is most precious to you from being ravaged by whoever happens to pass by – and that includes you! It is limit-setting to others, as well the main tool for self-discipline. It is also a prerequisite for forging a trusting, healthy relationship with yourself. Why? Because a "no" to them is a resounding "yes" to you! How affirming and refreshing! It frees you up to take care of yourself, right this moment. No, I cannot come over, I feel tired. No, I am not able to do this, I don't feel comfortable with it. Saying no buys you self-esteem and confidence, because instead of abandoning yourself, and agreeing to something that doesn't sit well with you, you are advocating for yourself. This way, you will like yourself, and never feel alone, because you will always have You as a best friend and ally.

Tired? Say "no" to activity, and rest. Grumpy? Watch a funny movie. Sad? Cry and talk to someone. These and such are our needs, as they arise and subside with the breath of each moment, the ebb and flow of everyday life. And you were going to miss it, because of an errand you – or they - think is more important. Than what? You?

We typically acquire the ability to say no in adolescence, when we are biologically compelled to separate and differentiate from our parent figures. This is how we become our own person, how we develop a sense of our own Self. We do it by going out on a limb, and take the risk of getting kicked out of the nest, or just plain yelled at for a few years until we figure out how to do this without being rude. Did you have the luxury to do this as a teenager?

Often, in stressed families (for instance with a single, addicted, or ill parent) children do not get the green light to go ahead, and do this. Early attempts are squelched by the parent(s) because the family does not have the extra energy to deal with the stress the separation process creates. Separating – i.e. rebelling, saying no - could bear some catastrophic consequences, like the family disintegrating, or someone relapsing into addiction, getting hurt, sick or even dying - obviously, not the kinds of chances a young teenager would take!

If you feel you missed your chance to learn saying no, take heart. You have that chance now, your learning only got postponed. You can start practicing here and now, every little time you don't feel you can say yes "with a singing heart". *Now* you have the opportunity and the necessary guidance to learn the necessary skills, by noticing your discomfort in real time, soothing yourself with it, and communicating with your body about your feelings and needs. If what it tells you is to speak up for yourself (as a need you have at this time), do it. Your body will provide you with the necessary motivation, as well as ammunition (i.e. energy) to help yourself.

If you were brought up with the domineering style of parenting you may feel like talking is "talking back". There is no disrespect in sharing your feelings and needs with another person. Not only that, telling it like it is represents the biggest favor you can give to others. It is like a road sign – one to your heart: it sets everyone up for getting safely to their destination, which is, believe it or not, to please you.

Do not underestimate the power of the WORD. Used appropriately it is a blessing, because it generates and upward spiral of positive energy, love, cooperation. Not used, or used inappropriately it will become a curse of self-reinforcing negativity, misunderstandings, and loneliness.

On this note, you might be interested in knowing that there are three styles of communication. My clients are always fascinated by this, because there is so much need for clarity and useful concepts to grasp what is going on in our relationships. (Not so) coincidentally, I will not be burdening you with too many new ideas here, because the three styles of communication happen to be the very same as the three styles of parenting.

The Three Styles of Communication

And the winners are: abusive, neglectful and caring. Okay, only one of those is the winner, the other two won't work. Abusive and neglectful are reactive. You remember from earlier chapters that reactivity is what you see in Nature, when an animal is in a life or death situation; they attack or they take flight, and this keeps them alive (for a while). In our human society reactivity is not adaptive behavior. We are practically never in a life or death situation; if and when humans are in a war, or famine, or epidemic, they must be reactive if they are to survive. Otherwise, it is safe to say that reactivity is not going to serve our survival, or thriving, but cause misunderstandings and destroy the cooperation we all depend on.

The assertive style is the only communication style conducive to cooperation, and therefore thriving.

We learn how to communicate mostly in childhood, from observing others, and from our own experience regarding what works. Communication styles can be un-learned and re-learned. If necessary, so they must be if we are to be healthy and well-adjusted.

The Aggressive Style of Communication: RAMBO (Reactive, Aggressive, Mean, Blaming Others)

This style is wrought with negativity and judgment. Put the shoe on the other foot: if it would hurt you, it most probably hurts others. When you use this style of communication you will not get what you need, instead, you will be misunderstood. What the other party will hear is that she is stupid, incompetent, and not good enough for you. This is obviously not what you intended to say, other than for the benefit of a quick anger-discharge. What you really meant to say is what you need from the other to feel better (e.g. love, attention, appreciation, soothing), so he may give it to you, and everybody wins. When you use any of the following your communication style is abusive, and you *will* be misunderstood:

- Blame
- Criticism
- Sarcasm
- Judgment
- Putdown
- Labeling
- Bullying
- Cursing
- Humiliating
- Yelling
- Name calling
- Meanness
- Threatening
- Generalizations ("You always (never)____"
- Stating the obvious
- Verbosity

What you really meant to say is that you are upset, and that you need the other to do something different. Unless you say what it is, you are NOT communicating, only hurting the other – and miss your chance of being helped.

When my daughter Julia was 14 she and I had a predilection for those oh-so-good mother-teenage daughter fights. Once as I was scolding her, and she was yelling at me, finally, she looked at me with huge tears in her eyes, and shouted: "What do you want from me?". I froze, mortified by the sudden realization that I never actually told her that. Then, after a moment of thought I said "I want you to clean your room once a week, talk to me nicely, and call me when you are late". And then, a miracle happened: she said "OK!" with a shrug. And that was that.

The aggressive style is likely to provoke lots of conflicts, because anger generates anger. The only thing your partner will hear is that he is not good enough for you, which destructs his self-esteem, as well as the relationship itself. He will hear nothing about your needs and feelings. You will be misunderstood each and every time you put your RAMBO on: not a good thing for establishing safety in intimate relationships.

In its mildest form, aggressiveness is verbosity, and stating the obvious. When you say "you came home at 5 and then put on the TV and you did not eat dinner with me" you are stating the obvious. Everyone present knows that is in fact what happens as a rule. So? What's it to you, the other will think, and feel hurt and confused. They will scramble to figure out what they are doing wrong, and more importantly: what it is that you want them to do instead?? When you state the obvious, or when you use too many words, and beat around the bush, you are not only mystifying your audience, you are also, in actuality, aggressing upon them. Verbosity, too is the hotbed for misunderstandings because, just like too few words, it is missing a vital component: information. The other will desperately try to fill in the blanks - most frequently with their own worst fears. What is your worst fear in your close relationships? The same as everybody else's, I reckon: that you are not good enough, and that they don't love you. And that is exactly what the other "hears" when you use too many words, or otherwise do not say how you feel and what you need from them.

The RAMBO style of communication is a serious risk-factor for addictions, violence against one's self or others, as well as antisocial and criminal behavior. The only redeeming aspect in this style of communication is that it is active – a prerequisite, one might say, when it comes to wanting to get your needs met.

The Passive Style of Communication: BAMBI (Busy, Absent, Muffled, Barely Involved)

For BAMBI here we don't mean the sweet little fawn, but a much less innocent style of communication that is intended to avoid conflict when there is stress. The person elects not to share her feelings and needs with her significant others, perhaps for lack of faith that she can be heard, understood and taken care of. Sometimes people become avoidant because they don't want to be like mom or dad who was a RAMBO. Unfortunately, it does not work. The recipient(s) of such style of communication are unavoidably left feeling neglected, not good enough and lonely - just like the person using this style. The message is that she does not trust you, you don't matter, and that you are not good enough – most probably not what the sender intended. Nobody gets what they need, and the silence is screaming. Imagine the passive style of communication as a person walled in by bricks saying:

- Cold shoulder
- Absence
- Physical distancing
- Closed off body language
- Changing subjects
- Small talk
- Silence
- Isolation
- Passivity
- No preference
- Expressionless
- No affection
- No feedback

Most divorces in the US are caused by BAMBI. It will leave problems un-addressed and relationships and feelings unresolved, which, in turn, exponentially increases the probability of getting depressed, anxious, addicted, or physically ill. The person using the BAMBI style will feel isolated and lonely, and people around him mistrusted, cut-off and inadequate. Everybody loses, because in lack of information there can be no cooperation. Divorces happen because of the accumulation of negative messages we fill the blanks with, leading to disconnect and mistrust. Everyone involved fills in the many "information blanks" - with what? Their worst fears, of course. Misunderstandings central – and all parties involved bleed from a thousand wounds.

Do you like to avoid conflict? It cannot be done. Conflict is a basic ingredient of Life, because it is a manifestation of change. As in the physical world, so in our lives everything changes at all times, and so the different parts need to renegotiate their relationship at each step of the way. Please talk to yourself about this, and convince yourself that there is nothing wrong with difference. The process of negotiating does not need to become negative or scary, even if in your childhood experience that is the way it was.

Remember this: the only way to keep the stress of change and renegotiating differences at a minimum is to be assertive.

By keeping silent you are just postponing the inevitable, while ladling more stress onto yourself and those around you.

Lack of clarity spells ambivalence and anxiety. Your partner leaving and going to a different room when you come home can mean a million different things, and you will be standing there desperately trying to guess what it means; anger, contempt, boredom, dislike, or even hate? Or did he have a bad day? As we will interpret the silence with our worst fears, we will unavoidably voice or act on our perception, as if it was reality, without getting a reality check by asking the other. Now, *that* is something to fear, because it will lead to more misunderstandings, resulting in conflict or more disconnect.

When you are not being heard because you are silent your will get frustrated (expecting the other to somehow read your mind). Sometimes people become vindictive in their frustration, and do things they *know* upset the other. This acting out behavior is called passive-aggressive. When this happens it is a downward spiral, because it generates more and more loss of trust and hope. Both parties are likely to feel exasperated and profoundly lonely.

The only redeeming factor in this communication style is that it is peaceful. Let us combine peace of BAMBI with the activity of RAMBO and we get ASSERTIVE, or caring communication. Assertiveness is always peaceful, cooperative, friendly, while active and relentless in seeking a resolution: the fulfillment of the needs of the parties involved. What is good for the goose is good for the gander! This is true even if asserting causes some transitory discomfort in the parties involved – until a consensus is reached.

The Assertive Style of Communication: CARE (Clear, Attentive, Responsive, Empathic)

In order to avoid subscribing to the RAMBO or BAMBI culture it helps to remember that your current partner, husband, wife, friend, or child is *not* the person from whom you learned them as a kid. You are probably projecting that parent onto this person. This is not only unfair, but also damaging to the relationship. Take responsibility for changing your style of communication into assertive. The others have become obsolete, effectively blocking you from having the safe and intimate relationships you seek.

Express yourself completely,
Then keep quiet.
Be like the forces of nature:
When it blows, there is only wind;

When it rains, there is only rain;

When the clouds pass, the sun shines through.

Lao Tzu

A lot of people have misgivings about assertiveness. Often it is confused with aggressiveness, though it could not be further from it. Aggression hurts, assertion helps and soothes fears. When you assert your feelings and needs you are actually doing people a favor; it is like the road signs that say "Boston". Without it people would not know what direction to go to get there. Voicing your feelings and needs are the road signs to your heart, saying: this is the way, to please this girl/boy. You can only please me if you know how, which can only happen if I tell you. Without me sharing what pleases me here and now, you would be guessing, and guessing wrong, nine times out of ten at best.

You want to cook up disappointment? Here is the recipe:

1. Take a pinch of "needing-something-from-the-other"
2. Add some "don't-tell-him-what-it-is"
3. Mix it with "he-can-tell-you-need-something-and starts-to-try-guessing-frantically"
4. Add a "blind-guess-based-on-what-she-would-need-in-such-circumstances"
5. BOOM! It is wrong! "Disappointment" is now ready
6. Serve by breaking a dish because you get mad at him for not giving you what you need
7. Decorate with him getting mad at you for getting mad at him...

MIND–READERS ANONYMOUS

Are You a Member?

The following is a partial list of rationales people use to not be assertive; please read each one carefully, then, in your mind, burn after reading:

- I did not know I could
- It's not the right time
- It's not the right place
- It's not that important
- It would be inconvenient
- It would be selfish
- It would be self-centered of me
- It's presumptuous to think it matters
- It's grandiose: I am not the center of the universe
- It's disrespectful
- I am on my own
- I don't want to burden anyone
- I should not depend on anyone for anything
- It's not polite to discuss/question/ask
- I should be compliant
- I must be good
- I must accommodate
- I must not expect others to make me happy
- I must be seen, but not heard
- I must grin and bear
- I must put up and shut up
- He/she would not understand
- He/she should know without me saying it
- If she/he really loved me I would not have to ask
- I don't really need that
- I should not think that
- I am not worth it
- I will get punished for asking

The only exception to the burning after reading would be:

It is not safe. If you feel you are in physical danger when you express a feeling or a need you are in an abusive relationship, and need to get help, pronto.

Assertiveness is the main tool in teaching and parenting people around you, so they can be good enough for you. It is the biggest favor. It is also...ready?

THE MAIN TOOL FOR SELF-CARE!

Without it you are giving up your most essential role in life: making it work, while shaping the culture you are living in.

Now, you might think you have been speaking your truth - but have you really? Are people in your life understanding you as evidenced by giving you what you need? If you have not been getting what you need in some important aspects of your life, it is safe to assume that you have been misunderstood.

Let us exclude for now the tiny, but implausible possibility that nobody loves you and they don't care, and/or they are stupid. What if they DID love you, DID care, and were SMART, but totally misunderstood you because of the way you did or did not speak your truth? It's okay to admit it, it's between us (I won't tell!). If this is the case, I am sure we can agree that is a setup for failure for anyone around you. In my native Hungarian there is a saying: "Not even a mother can hear a mute child".

So speak, my dear, and you shall be heard. Whether correctly or not depends on how you put it. If you blurt your feelings out they are going to sound like blame to the listener. On the other hand, only if you do speak can you even have the chance to get what you need. You might want to use your self-soothing techniques here. Do your best, I say, it's the best you can do!

My Kindhearted Reader, how I wish to embolden you to use your voice and your words to reach for everything you need. It is only when you ask that you receive - and nobody on this Earth is more worthy of receiving than you.

When Should I Be Assertive?

Consider these two factors:

1. As you notice how you feel (A), ask yourself how strongly you feel about this issue or situation. Trust your intuition! If it is a 7 or more on a scale from 0 to 10 it is time to assert yourself. If you did not, you would resent yourself and the others involved for not getting what you need. Spare this pain and SPEAK!
2. Ask yourself the three questions of the Buddha:
    -   Is it true?
    -   Is it necessary?
    -   Is it kind?

If the answer is "yes' to all three, by all means, SPEAK!
On this note: notice how gossip does not fulfill these criteria. Not a coincidence, since it is neither communication, nor assertiveness...

...And How?

Here are the basic guidelines:

1. Notice early when feeling upset (A)
2. Take a few deep breaths (B)
3. Say how you feel, using feeling words, and only I-statements (C) (Ask your body!)

4. Say what you need, specifically and positively (C)
5. Say nothing else!
6. If it matters to you (7 or more from 0 to 10) do not drop it!
7. Negotiate with the other party's needs until a resolution is reached.

You might want to post this on your fridge, it's that important!

<u>Say how you feel:</u> You can only say what you are aware of. This is where your ABC's come in handy. Notice where you feel the stress of any given situation in your body, and breathe into it. Then, ask the sensation about how you feel. The words and images that come up from that point of sensation are the truth of how you feel.

When you speak your feelings use "I statements", like "I feel ashamed, or worried, or small, or sad, etc." Any word on the Feelings List is safe and effective to use, because it will be immediately understood, and with compassion. Everyone is familiar with feelings, we all have them! Feelings are our common language – as opposed to thoughts, or judgments, which divide us.

Emotional intelligence requires using feeling words, because they lead to understanding and cooperation. Thoughts often lead to conflict and strife. Stay away from any phrase that includes the word "you". "I feel like you don't care" is not a feeling, it is a judgment... Same goes for "I feel as though you are <u>(fill in the blank)</u>. When you state your feelings like that you will be misunderstood, every time, in fact you will provoke a conflict, which is probably the last thing on your agenda. Don't waste your breath on unnecessary misunderstandings: speak your truth crisply, and precisely.

Also, given the circumstances, don't hesitate to elaborate briefly on what that feeling is like for you, e.g. what it reminds you of, why it is important, and to what degree. About the issue's importance you might say, this to me is an 8 on a scale from 0 to 10, because it reminds me, for instance, of when my Dad used to ignore me. Anything that is non-threatening but explains your part is welcome – in small doses! Too many words will get you in trouble. You do not want to be bogged down by what is, because the whole point is to move to what must happen in order for you to be well!

The reason why it is important to say how you feel is because without this piece of info the other may misconstrue your motives. If you need a cup of tea from your partner, and you do not say how you feel, they may take this as an attempt to control them, or to disturb them for some reason. However, if you start by saying you have a headache, for instance, they will instantly get the picture, and with a little luck, even make you that tea – despite of all the other things they were engaged in at the moment, just because love trumps all! Always remember that you matter, one, because you are loved, two, because we are all hard-wired to please each other. Our very survival hinges on this, so don't be shy about being assertive, you are doing everyone a favor!

What matters here is not the outcome (we will deal with the negotiating part later), but that you do your best as you go to be crisp and clear in your communication about your feelings and needs. This is the way to maximize the potential for a true connection between people.

Say what you need: In order to make sure you are understood you must be clear when you say what you need as well. It is essential to be specific, positive – and brief! If you say anything other than what you need, when, how and where, you will be, yes, you got it, misunderstood. Another breath wasted on the unworthy, you will conclude with a sigh of resignation. Instead, you want to collect instances of words being heard, and needs gratified. These become chips of experience that deposit in your psyche's love-bank, building harmony and peace within your heart and relationships.

For instance, you need more attention from your husband or wife. If you say, like so many, "You are never home, we never spend any time together, you just don't care about me" what you have at your hands is a fight, or, worse yet, silence. What works instead is to say how you feel, e.g. lonely, disconnected, sad, and what you need, e.g. "I need you to come home earlier from work, so we can spend some time together, at least three times a week. Can you do 5 o'clock?"

Putting it this way you are clear and specific, and positive with your needs, without raising defensiveness in the other.

> Kelly adores her husband of 15 years, and she is living in dread of his drinking habit that could ruin his health. Afraid of addressing this directly with him she performs summersaults to distract him from pouring another glass of wine. He is annoyed at her constant attempts to keep him busy (i.e. distracted from the booze), and has no clue why she is doing this – he thinks she wants to control him, like his mother did. This makes him want to drink even more. She would be better off directly addressing the problem in a loving and specific way, while getting the true importance of the issue on the table. If this does not work, it is time for some healthy limit-setting.

Being specific is very important also because when you put your needs in generic terms, like "I need you to care about me", you are in actuality insulting the other, because in their book they do care, and show you amply in their own way, assuming they are being good by you. She might think, for instance, that he feels loved, because she waits for him with a hot meal every night, while he might not feel loved, because the bedroom is cold. This is why requests must be specific in order to be understood and, hopefully honored. Of course, there is a pre-requisite for you to be able to do this:

TRUST YOUR OWN FEELINGS!

Once you have started asserting your feelings and needs, and you encounter resistance,

DON'T STOP!

Resistance is nothing but a lack of adequate understanding – so try to get your point across in a different way, cranking up your resolve. What you want is important to you, so stay the course! In this process, you will soon find that you have to stick with what matters to you and find more creative ways to persuade and remind the other about it. If you give up, the message is that you don't really care.

Your needs must also be negotiated and priorities established between partners as to whose needs will get met first. This takes time, patience, and energy. But if you think about it, would you rather get exactly what you want when you want it the way you want it, or get along, feel connected and cared about, and have peace by coming up with a livable compromise?

In summary, to be assertive, when you feel uncomfortable, or, for that matter, good, do say something, and do not blame the other in any way. Before you talk calm yourself down. If you let your anger seep out you will be misunderstood; why talk then? People's ears fall off when they feel threatened, so don't talk under the influence of intense upset feelings. The following rules are foolproof in making sure that what you mean to say will be received in exactly the way you intended, and that the conversation will resolve any conflict in fairness to both parties involved:

The Basic Rules of Healthy Communication

- No negative words, threats, blame, or sarcasm
- Say how you feel
    o Speak only of yourself

- o Use only feeling words
- o Explain why it is important to you
- o Say to what degree it matters to you (0-10)
- Say what you need
  - o Be specific
  - o Be positive
  - o Watch tone, verbiage, speed, volume
- If it matters, don't drop it! Say it differently, use examples
- STOP, and de-escalate if tone, verbiage, pace, volume, or body language bother you. Do not continue conversation until these have been corrected.
- One person at a time (first come, first serve)
- One issue at a time
- Negotiate! - stay positive, engaged, and don't stop until everybody is happy!
- Do not take it personally: each one of you has a right to your own preferences.

This may be another one begging to be put on your fridge!

Assertiveness, or effective communication is actual work, a labor of love that is worth every ounce of energy, because in the end you will feel understood, connected, and loved. If you do not currently have people in your life who are willing and able to do this with you (once they actually know how), seek, and you shall find!

If you have trouble communicating, you will find another exercise in the Appendix. If you are still finding it hard to communicate with yourself and others, please remember that a little professional help can give you just the boost you need.

Taking Things Personally: Boundaries

When you make it a strong habit not to take anything personally, you avoid
many upsets in your life. Your anger, jealousy, and envy will disappear, and
even your sadness will simply disappear if you don't take things personally.

Don Miguel Ruiz

Boundaries are trusting your gut feelings about when you are being hurt, and
when you are not, or what is your job, and what is not, what you have control
over and what you don't. They represent the fence around your garden that
preserves your energy and your safety.

Taking things personally – like someone expressing their feelings - means your
boundaries need some work. When you take things to heart, your feelings
distract you from hearing the true message, usually that the other is hurting.
You will then actually hi-jack the issue, and run with it, when you were not
supposed to be the focus of it in the first place! I hear this often from teens
who cannot talk to parents about their problems, because it turns into the
parent worrying, rather than the kid getting guidance.

Abuse and neglect, any shade of them temper with our boundaries, our sense
of what is good and healthy. If you received such treatment as a child, you
are probably having a hard time trusting your feelings, and you may have an
over-active mind engaged in trying to figure out others' motives. Because of
this distraction from your gut-feelings you will put up with too much, or too
little pain (physical or emotional).

The only way you will be able to tell someone to stop hurting you and really
be heard is if you do not take their behavior personally. By this I mean that if
you think it is all about you, that they are *trying* to hurt you (which may be

the case once in a thousand, when you run into your garden variety mean bastard!), this will make you shake in the knees, disarm you, because you yourself are not so sure whether or not you deserve the abuse.

Taking things personally makes you reactive - that is passive or aggressive. It will make you want to run or fight for your life will mute you, literally. This is because whether or not you say or do something while feeling reactive, you will NOT be heard, or you will be misunderstood. Either way, you might as well be mute. The only way to actually be heard and understood is by being assertive, and this requires that you remain calm, that is responsive under the duress of feeling hurt or stressed.

I know, don't tell me, this is much easier said than done. But hear me out, because this is really important:

Anything anyone says or does is about them, and not about you.

People talk and act on their own feelings, their own thoughts, their own history, and needs, and fears, and desires. Even though they might target YOU personally, it still has NOTHING TO DO WITH YOU – well, unless you know from several different people's feedback that your behaviors are hurtful or inappropriate in some ways. Even then, their words or actions are certainly not a personal attack on you, but a natural consequence for what you do or say, a mirror of sorts. Even then, you can only learn and change if you are not reactive. Short of such a pattern rest assured that words, actions and behaviors from others are simply an expression of how they feel about themselves, rather than about you. You are just reminding them of their internal conflicts, but that does not mean you did anything wrong!

Let me show you the list of all the reasons why people say or do hurtful things:

1. They feel upset in some way, for reasons that are, and shall remain a mystery to you: hurt people hurt people!

2. They are triggered by your behavior or words, meaning you just pushed a "button" in their body memory that you did not know was there (i.e. it's not your fault!);

3. You just reminded them of someone else they do not like (e.g. their mother used to say the same thing when she was angry);

4. They had a fight with someone else, discharging frustration onto you;

5. They did not like their breakfast, or got up on the wrong side of the bed;

6. – 1,784 Other personal reasons (their history, physical state, mental state, relational state, sexual state, political, economic, spiritual, state, in general the state of their state)

1,785. You.

Another way of thinking of this is that some people have fleas, and when they come close to you, a flea or two may jump on you. This is nothing personal, fleas jump. Just brush them off, and move on. Don't be reactive, don't think they tried to hurt you. They just are, and do what they do, even when they are not around you. Will you remember this the next time you are taking something personally?

If you are reactive to another person's words, look inside of you to see why that might be.

1. Do they remind *you* of something that happened to you in the past?

2. Could *you* be projecting your own fears, worries, or thoughts onto this person that really belong to someone else?

3. Could you be the one who treats you like this, and you are angry about it?

This will help you to address and, hopefully, resolve any underlying reasons for your reactivity, reasons that ultimately may point to abuse, neglect, or trauma in your own past. You can then get to the root causes and resolve them, with professional help, if necessary.

It is no big surprise that the rules for firming up your boundaries are almost identical to the rules of assertiveness – hey, the truth is one and indivisible! Here they are:

1. Trust your gut feelings of discomfort;
2. Soothe yourself as soon as feeling stress;
3. Ask yourself how you are feeling and what you need;
4. Say it to the other person;
5. If you are not heard, say it differently;
6. If you are still not heard, and if you feel unsafe, remove yourself from the situation;
7. Do not do what makes you feel unhappy, stressed, or uncomfortable (e.g. don't say "yes" if it does not sit well with you!);
8. Do exactly what you need from yourself in order to feel better.

FOURTH STEP: D: Your Do's and Don'ts

GOAL: To reinforce our commitment to, and faith in ourselves by following through with the appropriate actions, decisions and words.

Beautiful words don't put porridge in the pot.
Botswana Proverb

We have gone through three steps, and now you know how to tap into the wellspring of information that is your body. Awareness, self-soothing and communication open the door to well-being. **D**, or doing what it takes, actually delivering to the promise is the climax: it transforms.

D is made of two parts:

1. Do what you need (bring in the love)
2. Do not do what hurts you (set proper limits)

Remember the two things that make for positive parenting? They are the same for self-parenting as well: be loving and restrictive.

Loving means taking care by listening to feelings and needs. Since we know that needs are Nature's dictates, and thus, non-negotiable, to meet them is also a mandate – if we really mean to be well. This is how love – including self-love – is *not optional.*

Some of the basic requirements for giving yourself love are the bedrocks of health, and as such, no-brainers. Still, sometimes we forget what they are:

-   plenty of sleep
-   healthy food
-   exercise
-   rest
-   positive company
-   positive self-talk   .
-   meaningful activities.

If during the step C you receive information from your inner Self about any of these, make sure you listen; would you call a parent "good" if he did not provide for these?

Jeff said that there is a major heaviness in his body every time his wife asked him to do something; he feels paralyzed. He had no idea why (of course, I did not either). As he asked his body (the heaviness) how he felt, the thing that jumped out was "HUNGRY". He was shocked, this never occurred to him. As it turns out, he never ate during the day, was starving and did not even know it! No wonder his body did not want to move to do yet another thing. It told him to EAT, for God's sake!

Limit Setting means setting healthy boundaries to, and disciplining the one you love – in this case: you. If you are wondering when in the world it is appropriate to set limits for yourself, the criteria are simple but strong. When it comes to jeopardizing your health or your safety the answer is a resounding NO! Make sure you mean it, too, do not come back on your word, consistency is a must in good parenting!

In your (C), Communication with your Self you may have received information about what it is you must stop doing. These things are generally the ones you know deep down that are bad for you, like hanging with the wrong crowd, staying in a hurtful relationship (after you gave it your all to communicate your needs – see assertiveness), or putting poisons in your body.

In your (D), Delivery to the promise you made to your Self be careful to lock yourself into a system of rewards and consequences that really work to motivate you to make it happen. Give it some thought, and make your system effective by tweaking the "strings" in a way you cannot out-weasel. Remember, firm limits are indispensable for your health and safety, the very bases of survival.

However many holy words you read,
however many you speak,
what good will they do you if you do not act on them?
Buddha

During the "interview" process your body informs you of the specifics of exactly what you need to do, when, how, with whom, and how often (WWWHHH). You must trust this information with your life: it *is* your life. *This* is the truth, and none other, even if Joe Shmo says otherwise; even if you are afraid; even if you disagree; even if _____ (fill in the blank). So, are you going to take this seriously? If so, don't stop short of accomplishing what you promised, down to the last detail.

Let's get down to it:

1. Take out your phone, your calendar, and plug these tasks in, making them as sacred as the next chore you have down (I don't know about you, but except for breathing, I will only do what is written in my schedule);
2. Set reminders. Send yourself and e-mail or text. Put yellow stickies on your bathroom mirror, or dashboard, or wherever you can't help but see it. You know, the way you would with something you *really* don't want to forget or miss (if it is really important I, for one, write it on my palm). Then,
3. Do it. Scheduling will help you to put your commitment into actions. Good intentions are not sufficient here (in fact, the road to Hell is paved with good intention, as they say). Talk is cheap. Deeds are called for.

Promises are like the full moon,
if they are not kept at once
they diminish day by day.
German Proverb

While you are learning the good habits of delivering to the promises you make to your Self it might also be helpful to have a reward system. If you perform this task by such and such date the reward is _____ (make it small, affordable, meaningful: a gold star will do!)

Conversely, if you function better under the threat of a consequence, lock yourself into delivering by setting one. An appropriate consequence is not a punishment, rather something that is good for you but you have been avoiding, e.g. calling someone to resolve something difficult, or going to the gym.

Undoing Obstacles

If you cannot even imagine you doing what it takes to feel better, there might be an emotional hurdle in the way. It is time to do another round of A-B-C-D in order to undo that obstacle:

1. Pay **A**ttention to how you feel when you think of this task; find its location in your body, and let yourself feel it;
2. **B**reathe into it, soothe yourself with it;
3. **C**ommunicate with it:
   - How do I feel?
   - What do I need to do, or say, or be like to feel better? What will it take?
4. **D**o it!

This quick process will undo any emotional of cognitive obstacle in the way of you helping yourself.

Now get back to the original tasks, and make sure your perform them. It helps to involve people around you, by telling them about what you plan to do and when. Accountability, people! It will keep you honest, and, above all, true to yourself.

Remember, it is worse to not keep a promise you made than to not promise in the first place. Once you paid attention, and heard the truth of what you must do it is imperative that you find a way to deliver it. Otherwise, it is a tease, the one thing that will discredit you in your own eyes. It will lead to disappointment in yourself, and negative self-talk, which will further deflate your energy and self-esteem. Your subconscious, or Inner Child is always watching, taking notes of how reliable and safe you are.

Since it is your goal to forge the most trusting relationship with your Self, beware the temptation to ignore a promise. Once broken, you will have to work twice as hard to replenish the trust between your IC and your IP. Undoing any obstacles in your way – whether emotional or physical – will help you ensure that the trust building stays in progress.

> *Although she was well aware of her feelings and needs Pat, a physical therapist was never able to reach for what she really needed: a better paying job, a good relationship, and caring for her physical appearance. The reason was a hidden one: she did not want to break the rule of his family about staying put. The messages she grew up with were "you are no better than others", "don't stick your neck out", and "who do you think you are?", and "don't be a Pollyanna". She felt paralyzed and guilty about listening to her feelings. She had to deliberately give herself permission to have feelings, and really mean it, before she could think and act positively on her needs.*

Life is continuous process of decision making and then acting. Conscious or not, the next action is the outcome of a choice. We always do something, even when we do nothing, because it is a choice on how to proceed. Make this a conscious process. Wake yourself up to the true motivations behind your choices and actions – especially the ones impacting the course of your life. With awareness, you will know whether you are acting out of fear - a big no-no! - or out of need and desire. Choose to act on the latters, and make them a priority.

You see, there are two modes of being, in fear, or in love. Fear is the mother of guilt, anger, shame, worry, and anxiety. Fear is reactionary. If you base your actions on these feelings you are not reaching for what you need, but, instead, you give in and cultivate the very same feelings. (The only exception is if you are in real danger, in which case reaction is what is called for.)

Doing what it takes to feel better does not mean you abstain from tasks that you don't like! It simply means you are mindful of your feelings, and do them in collaboration with your Inner Child, while still parenting yourself. It's okay to level with him, asking for collaboration in exchange for playtime later, or to give in to her, by delaying the task to a time when you feel more up to it.

Choose living in love. Love engenders listening, acceptance, presence, tenderness, compassion, sharing and trust. When you feel sad, or hurt you are also guided by love. Base your actions on your desires and needs, the very forward pulling energies your body is programmed with.

My Dear Reader, be your "knight in shining armor", and bring in all the good you crave in your life. Awareness and understanding open the door (A, B, and C); PRACTICE transforms!

Exercise 1: Homework

1. Divide a sheet of paper vertically in three columns;
2. In the first, write a list of the "issues" in your life;
3. Arrange them from most to least important or impactful;
4. In the second column write next to each what you can do about it short term and long term, specifically. (Grieving is also an act, and there is professional help for it, too);
5. In the third column write WHEN you will do that, specifically, to the month, day, and hour, and then

6. Plug it into your calendar; you may even set alerts;
7. DO IT!

The main homework that will help you along in achieving and maintaining health and balance is the Authenticity Process itself. Do it every day religiously, just like you would check in with your child each day about how he is doing. This will ensure constant connection with your True Self, and galvanize positive relationships and experiences throughout.

If you have trouble delivering to the promises you made to yourself, you will find another exercise for this in the Appendix.

Not the maker of plans and promises,
but rather the one who offers faithful service in small matters.
This is the person who is most likely to achieve what is good and lasting.
Johann Wolfgang von Goethe

Exercise 2: Vision Board

In order to achieve any goal you must have a vision of it first. We always imagine what we will do before doing anything. This is what in yoga they call "setting your intention". Set your intention on what you would like to see happening in your life by creating a Vision Board.

1. Take a large sheet of paper, pens, markers, and, if you like, magazines, and glue;
2. Write words and draw pictures on the sheet that express your desires, and arrange them in space in a way that makes sense to you, filling up the sheet of paper;

3. If you have magazines, you can also cut out words and pictures -selecting them intuitively - that express your vision on any level: materially, emotionally, relationally, etc.

4. Put the board in a place you can see it often; by glancing at the words and images they will become subconscious messages that you will be likely to carry out!

If you are having a hard time with this, you can always ask for help.

Summary of the ABCD Exercises

Here is an outline of the Authenticity Process, for your daily use. The point is to be diligent in doing your ABCD's each day, in order to carve it into your subconscious until it becomes your automatic mechanism.

A:

Pay <u>ATTENTION</u> to how your body feels by:

1. Grounding
2. Switching off the Mind
3. Balloon Technique
4. Body Scanning
5. Accepting self-talk/affirmations

B:

<u>BREATHE</u> into the sensation, BE with it

1. Belly Breathing
2. Safe Place Imagery
3. Positive Self-Talk

4. Affirmations
5. Positive Thinking

C:

<u>COMMUNICATE</u> with your Self

1. How am I feeling?
2. What do I need to do, say, or be like to feel better?

<u>COMMUNICATE</u> with Others = Assertiveness

1. Say how you feel
2. Say what you need

D:

<u>DO</u>

1. Homework
2. Practice ABCD

Here is a "sequence of events" of sorts. See if there are any points where you get stuck, and find the appropriate exercises to undo it:

(A)Sense → Notice → Accept →(B) Breathe → Feel → Self-soothe → (C) Ask yourself re: Feelings → Ask yourself re: Needs → Express your feelings → Express your needs → Ask for help → (D) Do what helps you...and the cycle starts over.

CONCLUSION

Take It with You

"Our deepest fear is not that we are inadequate. Our deepest fear is that we are powerful beyond measure. It is our light, not our darkness that most frightens us. We ask ourselves, 'Who am I to be brilliant, gorgeous, talented, fabulous?' Actually, who are you not to be? You are a child of God. Your playing small does not serve the world. There is nothing enlightened about shrinking so that other people won't feel insecure around you. We are all meant to shine, as children do. We were born to make manifest the glory of God that is within us. It's not just in some of us; it's in everyone. And as we let our own light shine, we unconsciously give other people permission to do the same. As we are liberated from our own fear, our presence automatically liberates others."

Marianne Williamson

SHRINKSTER: A Therapist in Your Pocket

Feeling stressed, worried, or just plain blah? You are now ready and able to get quick fixes that work, because through diligent practice you have acquired the necessary skills. "Shrinkster" is a shortened version of the A-B-C-D protocol, quick technique to help you out in a pinch, almost like a tiny therapist that is always with you. But don't get too confident; chances are you may start skipping a step here and there, thinking it's okay. It is not. Believe me, I know from experience, that when you skip a step – or even part of a step – it is because it does not come easy, and not because you are too good at it! So please watch for the points that want to be ignored, and program yourself to keep "good form". Remember, each element in this process is indispensable for achieving organic connection with your true source.

Here are the steps:

1. As you go through your day, check in with your body regularly, but especially before making any decisions, or promises;
2. Notice where the spot of highest sensation is in your body;
3. Zero in on it, take a deep breath into it, and send it a nod of approval or acceptance. Smile at it with love, and tell yourself "I have a right to feel, and it is safe for me to feel. I am now going to listen to what it is trying to tell me!"
4. Now, ask that sensation the two questions, 3-4 times each, and take (mental or written) notes of the subtle answers you are getting:
   - How am I feeling?
   - What do I need from myself to feel better? What do I need to say, do, or be like?
5. Do it!
6. Re-check the spot of the original sensation. If it is still there with the same intensity, repeat steps 1-5: you may have missed what really matters.

To enhance your experience, you can visit my website www.center4authenticliving.com for a short you-tube video that will lead you through this exercise.

Another quick way to take care of yourself is to watch your energy throughout the day. Notice its different qualities: is it choppy, strong, weak, even, soft, or rough? Pay attention, breathe, and do what it takes to massage it into a more comfortable flow. Also, by all means, gage your level of activity according to your level of energy.

Many people live life pushing, driven, fast. We are often evaluated, especially at work, according to our "performance". Be careful not to use this to measure your worth. You may be driven at work, however do not try this at home! Energy is your life force, your greatest asset, or resource. Everything we think of as a resource, like time, money, or connections is a representation of this underlying supply of energy. Do not spend every dollar you have, stash some of it for a rainy day (if you don't, this might be an indication of you relationship to your Self, to your energy, and that you might need to re-think your "expenditures"). By the same token, do not spend all the energy you have in a day, and squeeze yourself dry by evening time. Leave your battery 30-40 percent full by the end of the day: you need this reserve for emergencies, for optimal immune function, as well as to ensure optimal immune function, and to maintain your joy.

Joy: Living from the Overflow

Joy is not a special gift, cherry on top, or a luxury. It is our natural state, one we were all born with. It is the feeling that bubbles up automatically when you feel replenished. When life does not feel like joy or peace overall, or in the present moment, it is a signal that you are off course, and you must do something to correct that. My mother used to say "don't do it, unless you can do it with a singing heart!" I take that to heart, and because I do, my heart sings – and so will yours, when you take this advice. Feeling joyful, content, or peaceful are Nature's signals that all is well, stay the course, there is nothing to do. When your batteries are full, your energy is replenished you cannot help but spread the wealth: patience, a helping hand, a smile, kindness, acceptance, and compassion with others. This is living from the overflow.

Joy is not the same as pleasure, it is a lot more. Pleasure (a purchase, a ride, a travel, a gift, or sex, or good food) can contribute to our joy, however it is different from joy in that it is temporary, and it dissipates as soon as the triggering agent is gone. Joy is a state of mind, of presence and appreciation that you can cultivate by simply allowing yourself to experience it. Soon, it will become your modus operandi, just the way you are in this world. In order for joy to infuse our soul we need inner peace. Without inner peace the joy of the moment will not "stick" as a subconscious deposit, but flee as quickly as it arrived.

The key to inner peace is to have a positive relationship with your Inner Child – i.e. your feelings, that loving self-parenting.

Everything is about the way you feel.
Practice scenarios that feel good — and never mind reality.
Reality is only a brief moment in time that you keep repeating.
Esther Hicks / Abraham

I am sure you are pretty clear by now that this present moment is where health, authenticity, and well-being are to be found, because feelings flow in the moment. Many of us, however, forget to be in it, so as to take advantage of the constantly reoccurring chance to parent ourselves.

In order to cultivate joy, don't think anything fancy now, just picture yourself in your bed, waking up in the morning. Let yourself luxuriate in the warmth of your blanket, the pause before the day starts. When you are having a meal, smell your food, and give yourself a moment to really savor it with all your senses. Let the experience run through your body – in its simplicity and subtlety it is pure medicine! In fact, let these subtle positive energies saturate your system throughout the day, by allowing yourself to revel in the moment - any moment. These are pills of joy that will deposit in your subconscious and inspire happy thoughts. They, in turn will have you find more of these experiences. This is what I call cultivating joy. It is not something you seek out. It is something you allow into your experience, by virtue of being mindful.

When you recover or discover something that nourishes your soul
and brings joy, care enough about yourself to make room for it in your life.
Jean Shinoda Bolen

As you go through your day you can soak up the good inherent in each moment, like a little bee, suckering out the nectar of every flower. Then, when you feel a little off, do reach for what you need, the next *healthy* thing that will help you feel just a little better. When we get our needs met the body relaxes, the mind eases, and with all the tension of needing gone we become content and open – open to receive and absorb the positive energy that surrounds us. This is the natural state of joy – the ones babies feel after they are taken care of. Coincidentally, that is when they smile: an expression of how they feel.

When you have a lot to do, start with a meal.
South American Proverb

Stop and soak up the good in each moment: this is practicing presence. It comes with the quality of "being", as opposed to "doing".

Give yourself consistently the gift of just being: each moment, each hour, a time set aside each day to just be, each weekend, to rest and replenish your energies, and each season, with time off from work. Make it a priority to cultivate joy, by "slipping into the gap" (as Deepak Chopra says) between two thoughts or activities. What you cultivate becomes habit, which brings forth more of the qualities you want in your life

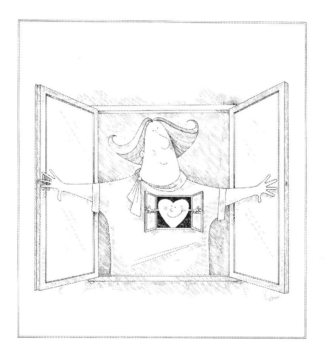

You must be deliberate in your joy-allowing. In order to make and keep it a regular in your life your active cooperation is necessary. Parent yourself well; make sure that you are "tethered" to your Inner Child's feelings, and fulfill her needs. As you know, she talks through your body's signals that inform instantly, correctly, authoritatively. Over time, you can learn to instantaneously correct any imbalance, so that you feel good most of the time. Feeling good while paying attention to it is what they call mindfulness: this practice recreates and reinforces itself. Less for *you* to do! Hallelujah!

You are not to allow struggle, strife, pushing, forcing, or effort into your life on any level (except for the caveat below), because the energy these represent are hurtful to your relationship to yourself, to your Inner Child. Also, you may get so used to it (and we get used to anything we do enough times) that you may lose awareness of your healthy sense of discomfort with them!

The only time you are to indulge in such stances is if the emotional reward they promise outweighs the emotional cost: your Inner Child begrudging your Inner Parent for rough handling. You be the judge, but be very careful!

How do you allow joy into your life, you might ask. I can think of a few ways to do this:

1. Unburden your schedule;
2. Try to accept the facts of life (illness, death, changes);
3. Give yourself permission to be joyous;
4. Notice the positives and think good thoughts each day;
5. Do positive things (help others, play, move, etc.)
6. Let go of the things you cannot control;
7. Focus on the present moment;
8. Take care of yourself (ever heard of ABCD?)
9. Be responsive to stress;
10. Front-load your days with joy (do not postpone it to vacation time or retirement, or when everything is done);
11. Catch yourself thinking "Let me get this over with", stop, and refocus on the good before resuming that task;
12. Pay attention to feeling good and soak it up deliberately.

Why not make it a habit to think: "Joy is my mandate; cultivating joy is my main job in the world. It is the single energy that replenishes me, so I can feel good and spill it over onto others".

Why not make up your mind about joy – why not decide that it is not only allowed into your life, but also welcomed, accepted, readily integrated? Do not resist it. Remember the chapter about your baseline of happiness? *Make joy your baseline*. Cultivate it, get used to it.

Many people profess that if you allow yourself to feel good you are setting yourself up for disappointment, because it will certainly pass. Consider this: living in the spirit of fear you taint with negativity even what is good. Truth is, there will be stress; however, if and when it strikes you will be better equipped to deal with it if you are fundamentally cultivating a positive, open and loving stance in life. Keeping yourself in a positive vibration will ensure that you have a strong "emotional immune system".

Massage yourself into making space for tolerating feeling good. Be deliberate about reaching for that higher vibration we call joy. Often we crave more fun, or peace, or adventure, but don't reach for it, as if it was normal to feel less than good enough. Maybe it was your normal, previously. That was then, and this is now; kick in the new rule, and practice it.

When it comes to the moments or periods of enjoyment stay open, present and positive, just like in the times of pain and discomfort. It is not only okay, but necessary to massage one's Self into allowing good feelings, and better, and then even better. There is no limit to how good one should feel. Existence is a concert of joy, where everything is a celebration of life force. In fact, *joy is our primal state, one we must safeguard by allowing it into our experience as often as possible and to the greatest degree we can muster.*

The goal in life is to minimize stress.

Vera Maros

Feeling naturally good and joyful is the measure for health. As much as you can help it, make it a sport to only do things as long as they feel like fun or joy, or at least comfortable. When you stop feeling that way - or never even started - drop what you are doing, do not forge ahead, twisting your arm into feeling bad. Instead, check in with yourself about what you DO need to feel better, and do it. Then, take notice of that feeling! Let it set a precedent, something you will blindly repeat again, and again.

You must create a blueprint of joyousness in your system, on a cellular level, by

- allowing yourself to experience it, and then by
- taking notice, and smiling upon it.

This way, you are likely to replicate the experience, without contaminating it with some bad feeling, or thought, and you will create a new automatic pilot of living in joy.

Joy is life, and life is joy, and it is supposed to *feel* like joy, no matter who says what! Watch your kids, or your pets, and you will see. We talk and discuss and do a lot, but we don't live enough. Come alive with the energy of your joy spontaneously emerging from your being, just by allowing yourself to be and go with the flow of your own feelings. Joy will come on the heels of you letting yourself feel whatever it is you are feeling – even pain. You see, we feel good when we don't try to control our feelings, but flow with them. You are either open, or closed. When you shun a bad feeling, you are closing yourself down to the good ones as well. You know how it is when you cry (and I hope you do sometimes), and people want to help by saying "stop crying!" Isn't that frustrating, that they want to interrupt something that feels good to you?

What's wrong with shining, anyway? We owe it to ourselves, as well as to others around us to unfold our colors and gifts, like a beautiful flower, for all to enjoy, don't you think? What's wrong with a little razzle-dazzle?

Expand yourself, my dear, breathe, it's all good, and so are you! No more shrinking in the shadows, hiding from the very light that you are. Let your light shine, nourished continually by your appreciation, compassion and love for your Self, expanded from your core to others and Life itself.

The Beginning

Appendix

Exercises to prepare for A-B-C-D

1. You Baseline of Unhappiness

- To what degree do you feel bad in your own skin? 0-10
- Take a fresh look at this, and accept your first, intuitive number as the true answer. Then, let yourself feel the pain of it; it will help motivate you to make a change!
- To what extent are you willing to tolerate feeling bad in in a situation or in a period of time? 0-10
- Let yourself feel any anger or frustration that comes up here. This will help you to firm up your commitment to make the necessary changes in your relationship to yourself.
- What are the hidden benefits you are getting from feeling bad (or being put down or neglected by others)?
- Realize that we do not do anything that is not rewarding in some way, so let your answer be candid and thorough. This will enable you to reconsider your most fundamental motivations and attitudes regarding abuse and neglect.

    1. _____
    2. _____
    3. _____

- Do you REALLY need that reward? If so, is there another, healthier, more positive way you could get it?
  1. _____
  2. _____
  3. _____

Forgiveness and Affirmations.

- Is there something you should forgive yourself for?
  1. _____
  2. _____
  3. _____
- Imagine you Inner Child (or someone you truly love) in your place;
- Think, and understand that he or she could not do otherwise, because did not have the tools or resources to act differently;
- Give him or her your forgiveness – tell them!
- Tell your adult Self that you forgive yourself (this is best done in front of a mirror). Take your time, no matter what or how long it takes! This way you may start giving yourself permission to allow more positive energy into your emotional and physical space).
- "I always did the best I could with what I had." Had you known better back then, you would have done better, but you did not know better and/or did not have the resources to. You may not have had the information, supports, maturity or words to make better choices back then.

  Who can judge a child for stealing bread when he is hungry? Why should you judge yourself for trying to cope and survive a situation you should probably never have been put into in the first place? Forgive that younger self of yours, as you would forgive someone else in that situation. Unless you were the perpetrator, the abuser, there is absolutely no need, or redemption in carrying guilt or shame about what you did. (If you were a perpetrator, use the guilt as a motivator to make amends, and *then* shed the guilt).

- Let yourself grieve for that younger self of yours that got hurt. In the healing process it is instrumental that you allow yourself to feel your pain, and comfort yourself with it, as you would hold and comfort someone you love who is grieving. Have compassion for your younger, hurt self. Shunning him or her will only perpetuate the pain, or cause disconnect, which may result in depression or another illness.
- Repeat to yourself thirty times at awakening, and thirty times right before falling asleep at night:
- "I always do the best I can with what I have"
- "I am a good person, and I accept myself just the way I am"

More Exercises for A: Acceptance

1. **Gratitude List**
   At the end of each day write 10 POSITIVE statements each starting with:
   - I have _____
   - I love/like _____
   - I am _____

2. **Giving**
   Acceptance is openness, it is fluid and generous – therefore
   Practice gifting yourself and others (including with kind words), as a way of appreciating and allowing the energy to flow freely (ref. Deepak Chopra the Seven Laws of Spiritual Success)

3. **Meditation** helps to sink into the way you feel right now. It is acceptance in that it helps us to lean into what is, letting go of all control. This opening allows for the spontaneous resolution of whatever physical or emotional state we were in before the sit.

More Exercises for B:

1. **The Worry Antidote**
   - Sit comfortably, breathe deeply a few times, relax your body;
   - Imagine the *best case scenario* for the thing you are worried about
   - See it, hear it, smell it, taste it, feel it in every little detail, in every way. Take your time to focus and imagine this, and really live it!
   - Let yourself be absorbed in the experience of this positive outcome, and stay with it until you know deep inside that this outcome is simply unavoidable.
   - Amen!

2. **Cognitive restructuring (to talk yourself out of negative thoughts):**
   - Take a sheet of paper and divide it vertically in two parts
   - On the left, write down your first negative, frightful thought
   - On the right, write down why it is not so: convince yourself with all the right arguments you would use with someone you love
   - Continue on the left with the next thought
   - ...and on the right with the negation of that thought
   - Continue until there are persuaded out of each one of your negative thoughts.

3. **Sleeping Technique 1:**
   This technique will help if you are having a hard time falling asleep because of too many thoughts twirling in your head. The act of writing your concerns down along with their solutions will effectively place them outside of your system, onto the paper, which will keep them for you until the next day.
   - Take a sheet of paper, and divide it in three parts vertically;
   - In the left hand column make a list of ALL the thoughts in your head;

- Rank them according to importance or relevance by putting a number next to each;
- In the next column write next to each WHAT you will do to take care of it;
- In the third column write next to each WHEN you are going to take care of it;
- Good night!

4. **Sleeping Technique 2:**

This is a very powerful self-hypnotic technique to put yourself to sleep, whether when you first go to bed, or if you wake up during the night.

- Relax your body as you lay in bed, and take a few slo-o-o-ow breaths;
- Imagine 10 stairs going down;
- Tell yourself: "By the time I get to the bottom of these stairs I will be sound asleep"
- Start going down, saying ONE in your head ... and double your relaxation in your body;
- TWO... and double your relaxation again;
- THREE...doubling your relaxation again;
- Continue until...yawwwwn... (You may not even reach five!)

Exercise for C:

Journaling

Journaling is one of my favorite self-help tools, because it provides a "container" for the process of checking in with your Self. With pen in hand and paper in front of you have a lower risk of getting distracted from this vital practice.

I think any journaling is good, as long as it is not just listing the things that you did or that happened that day. When done properly, journaling will help to lower your stress by getting your feelings out of your body and onto the paper.

Therefore, you might want to:

- Let your Inner Child talk (in the first person);
- Use feeling words;
- Express all your feelings in detail, without getting into writing about others;
- Soothe yourself/your Inner Child with your feelings with kind, compassionate words; put things into perspective for her;
- Express all your needs;
- Make specific plans, in writing about when and what you will do to meet those needs.
- Write in your journal every day, preferably at the same time, so that this exquisite self-parenting tool may solidify into a habit.

Recommended Readings

A.

Radical Acceptance by Tara Brach
The Power of Now by Eckhart Tolle
Turning the Mind into an Ally by Sakyong Mipham
Loving What Is by Byron Katie

B.

Touching the Earth by Thich Nhat Hanh
You Can Heal Your Life by Louise Hay
Creative Visualization by Shakti Gawain
To Be Healed by the Earth by Warren Grossman
What to Say When You Talk to Yourself by Shal Helmstedter
The Art of Extreme Self-Care by Cheryl Richardson
Ask and It Is Given by Esther Hicks
Simple Abundance by Sara Breatnach

C.

Non-Violent Communication by Marshall Rosenberg
Communication Miracles for Couples by Jonathan Robinson
The Four Agreements by Don Miguel Ruiz

Your Perfect Right: A Guide to Assertive Living by Robert Alberti and Michael Emmons

When I Say No I Feel Guilty by Manuel Smith

D.

The 7 Habits of Highly Successful People by Stephen Covey

The Seven Spiritual Laws of Success by Deepak Chopra:

Think and Grow Rich by Napoleon Hill

General Readings:

Tao Te Ching by Lao Tzu (transl. by Stephen Mitchell)

Finding the Flow by Mihaly Csikszentmihalyi

The Evolving Self by Mihaly Csikszentmihalyi

Authentic Happiness by Martin Seligman

The Joy of Living by Jongay Mingyur Rinpoche

The Prophet by Kahlil Gibran

Creating a Charmed Life by Victoria Moran

The Bhagavad Gita

The Dhammapada - the Sayings of the Buddha

The Creation of Health by Carolyn Myss

The Soul is Here for Its Own Joy ed. Robert Bly

Meditation by Osho

Healing into Life and Death by Stephen Levine

Dreaming the Soul Back Home by Robert Moss

The Happiness Project by Gretchen Rubin

The Art of Happiness by the Dalai Lama

Lit from Within by Victoria Moran

The Artist's Way by Julia Cameron

The Wabi Sabi House by Robyn Griggs Lawrence

Bibliography

Ainsworth MD (1967). *Infancy in Uganda.* Baltimore: Johns Hopkins

Bakeman, R. & Gottman, J. M. (1986) *Observing Interaction: An Introduction to Sequential Analysis.* Cambridge: Cambridge University Press

Berne, E. (1964) *Games People Play: The Basic Handbook of Transactional Analysis.* New York: Random House

Bloom, D. & Brownell, P. (eds) (2011) *Continuity and Change: Gestalt Therapy Now.* Newcastle, UK: Cambridge Scholars Publishing

Bowlby J. (1969). *Attachment.* Attachment and Loss. Vol. I. London: Hogarth

Bowlby J. (1979). *The Making and Breaking of Affectional Bonds.* London: Tavistock Publications

Bowlby J. (1988). *A Secure Base: Clinical Applications of Attachment Theory.* London: Routledge

Brach, T. (2003) *Radical Acceptance.* New York: Bantam Books

Broderick, C. B. (1993) *Understanding Family Process: Basics of Family Systems Theory.* London: Sage Publications

Brownell, P. (2010) *Gestalt Therapy: A Guide to Contemporary Practice*. New York, NY, US: Springer Publishing

Dethlefsen, T. & Dahlke, R. (2002) *The Healing Power of Illness: Understanding What your Symptoms Are Telling You*. Vega Books

Freud, S. (1960) *The Ego and the Id*. New York: Norton

Gendlin, E. T. (1981) *Focusing*. New York: Bantam New Age Publications

Goleman, D. (1995) *Emotional Intelligence*. New York: Bantam Publications

Grossman, W. (1998) *To Be Healed by the Earth*. Cleveland, OH: Warren

Grossman School of Healing

Hay, L. (1999) *You Can Heal Your Life*. Hay House, Inc.

Hicks, E., Hicks, J. (2004) *Ask and It Is Given*. Carlsbad, CA: Hay House, Inc.

Hunter, R. (2005) *Hypnosis for Inner Conflict Resolution: Introducing Parts Therapy*. Wales, UK: Crown House Publishings

Jung, C. G. (1964). *Man and his Symbols*. Chicago: Ferguson Publishing Company

Kahlil Holmes J. (1993). *John Bowlby & Attachment Theory*. Makers of modern psychotherapy. London: Routledge

Karen R. (1998). *Becoming Attached: First Relationships and How They Shape Our Capacity to Love*. Oxford and New York: Oxford University Press

Levine, T. B-Y. (2011) *Gestalt Therapy: Advances in Theory and Practice*. New York, NY: Routledge

Maccoby, Eleanor E., and John A. Martin. 1983. Socialization in the Context of the Family: Parent-Child Interaction. In *Handbook of Child Psychology*, ed.

Paul H. Mussen. Vol. 4: *Socialization, Personality, and Social Development*, ed. E. Mavis Hetherington, 1–101. 4th ed. New York: Wiley.

Main, M., Solomon, J. (1986). "Discovery of an insecure disoriented attachment pattern: procedures, findings and implications for the classification of behavior". In Brazelton T, Youngman M. *Affective Development in Infancy*. Norwood, NJ: Ablex

Mipham, S. (2003) *Turning the Mind into and Ally*. New York: Riverhead Books

Prior V, Glaser D (2006). *Understanding Attachment and Attachment*

Disorders: Theory, Evidence and Practice. Child and Adolescent Mental Health, RCPRTU. London and Philadelphia: Jessica Kingsley Publishers

Perls, F. (1969) *Ego, Hunger, and Aggression: The Beginning of Gestalt Therapy*. New York, NY: Random House (originally published in 1942, and re-published in 1947)

Perls, F. (1969) *Gestalt Therapy Verbatim*. Moab, UT: Real People Press

Perls, F. (1969) *In and Out the Garbage Pail*. Lafayette, CA: Real People Press

Perls, F., Hefferline, R., & Goodman, P. (1951) *Gestalt Therapy: Excitement and growth in the human personality*. New York, NY: Julian

Perls, F. (1973) *The Gestalt Approach & Eye Witness to Therapy*. New York, NY: Bantam Books.

Truscott, D. (2010) Gestalt therapy. In Derek Truscott, *Becoming an Effective Psychotherapist: Adopting a Theory of Psychotherapy That's Right for You and Your Client*, pp. 83–96. Washington, DC, US: American Psychological Association

Rahula, W. (1974). *What the Buddha Taught*. New York: Grove Press

Rogers, C. (1961) *On Becoming a Person*. Boston: Houghton Mifflin Company

Staemmler, F-M. (2009) *Aggression, Time, and Understanding: Contributions to the Evolution of Gestalt Therapy*. New York, NY, US: Routledge/Taylor & Francis Group; GestaltPress Book

Tannen, D.(1986) *That's Not What I Meant!* New York: Ballantine Publishing Company

Tinbergen N (1951). *The Study of Instinct*. Oxford: Oxford University Press

Tolle, E. (1997) *The Power of Now*. Novato, California: New World Library

Walter, J. L. (1992) *Becoming Solution Focused in Therapy*. New York: Brunner/Mazel

Watson, J. C., Lietaer, G. (eds) (1998) *Handbook of Experiential Psychotherapy*. New York: Guilford Press

Watzlawick, P. (1967) *Pragmatics of Human Communication: A Study of Interactional Patterns, Pathologies, and Paradoxes*. New York: W. W. Norton & Company

Weissmark, Mona Sue & Giacomo, Daniel A. (1998). *Doing Psychotherapy Effectively*. Chicago: The University of Chicago Press

Whitfield, C. L. (1989) *Healing the Child Within*. Deerfield Beach, CA: Health Communications, Inc.

Woldt, A. & Toman, S. (2005) „Gestalt Therapy: History, Theory and Practice". Thousand Oaks, CA: Sage Publications